Fanatics and Fire-eaters

THE HISTORY OF COMMUNICATION

Robert W. McChesney and John C. Nerone, editors

A list of books in the series appears at the end of this book.

N

Fanatics and Fire-eaters

NEWSPAPERS AND THE

COMING OF THE CIVIL WAR

Lorman A. Ratner
and Dwight L. Teeter Jr.

UNIVERSITY OF ILLINOIS PRESS
URBANA AND CHICAGO

First paperback edition, 2004
© 2003 by the Board of Trustees
of the University of Illinois
All rights reserved
Manufactured in the United States of America
5 4 3 2 1 C P 5 4 3 2 1

∞ This book is printed on acid-free paper.

The Library of Congress cataloged the cloth edition as follows:
Ratner, Lorman.
Fanatics and fire-eaters : newspapers and the coming of the Civil War /
Lorman A. Ratner and Dwight L. Teeter Jr.
p.   cm. — (The history of communication)
Includes bibliographical references and index.
ISBN 0-252-02787-6 (cloth : acid-free paper)
1. United States—History—Civil War, 1861–1865—Causes.
2. Journalism—Political aspects—United States—History—19th century.
3. Press and politics—United States—History—19th century.
4. American newspapers—History—19th century.
5. United States—Politics and government—1849–1861.
6. United States—Social conditions—To 1865. I. Teeter, Dwight L. II. Title.
III. Series.
E459.R3125   2003
973.7'11—dc21   2002006415

Paperback ISBN 0-252-07221-9

For Paula Kaufman and Letitia Teeter

CONTENTS

PREFACE

We undertook this study because of our interest in two subjects. Along with many others, we wondered about the dynamic between ideas and actions that resulted in the American Civil War. We also wondered about what newspapers, which by the mid-1850s had become so numerous and so large in circulation as for the first time to become mass media, would reveal about the societal conflicts resulting in war.

From 1856 to 1861, the fabric of American society was torn by a series of events. Each event—described and fervently commented on in newspapers North and South—resulted in anger, fear, and hatred between and among segments of American society. No sooner would these emotions begin to subside when another inflammatory event would rekindle those ignoble emotions and add to them. We chose six events which, between 1856 and 1861, riveted national attention and generated great controversy. In chronological order, the events were the Brooks-Sumner caning incident of May 1856; the *Dred Scott* decision of March 1857; the debates over the Lecompton Constitution for Kansas during the winter of 1857–58; John Brown's raid at Harpers Ferry, Virginia, in the fall of 1859; Abraham Lincoln's election in November 1860; and the firing on Fort Sumter in April 1861. Each event was covered and commented upon in every newspaper in the land.

We selected a number of newspapers published in different parts of the country, newspapers representing differing political positions. Although many were published in cities, not all were urban. Some urban newspapers, notably Horace Greeley's circulation-leading New York *Tribune,* were either widely circulated or published weekly editions read across the country. Although we assume that newspapers must have influenced the opinions of those who read them, we have no way to measure that influence. Instead, we believe that the great value of newspapers was what they might reveal about the emotions and opinions of their readers. To stay in business and prosper, editors had to remain generally attuned to words and ideas that would attract the readers they sought.

Our reading of how those newspapers covered such events, whether in the descriptions chosen as news or in their editorializing, led us to conclude that views about slavery, in each case, ignited the controversy. It became equally obvious that concerns about the American Republic served as the fuel that fed the fire. Ever since the Revolutionary War, Americans had debated whether the paradox of slavery in a society dedicated to freedom should be tolerated, and, if not, could the issue be resolved without dismembering the Republic? From revolutionary times to the 1850s, concern about that paradox rose and fell. Public controversy would be quieted by compromise, only to surface again.

By 1856 debates over slavery were linked more dramatically than ever to the Republic's survival. In the coverage and explanation of the events we chose to study, almost every newspaper characterized the events either as evidence of a defense of or as an attack on the Republic. What the event might mean for the future of slavery was secondary. Participants in those events were characterized either as republican society's friend or its enemy.

The word *republic* seemed to have many meanings and to conjure up different images. It was used to refer to Americans' heritage, in particular to the Founding Fathers and the generation they led that sacrificed so mightily for freedom. When used as an adjective, "republic" described a perceived national character and the central attributes of American society, elements that made the society unique and superior to all others. Then there was a propensity to connect America's dramatic growth in wealth and world prominence with its embrace of republican values and institutions. Linking slavery with the survival of the Republic made the ultimate outcome of the debate over slavery of far greater concern to many more people than would have been the case had slavery alone been the subject of controversy.

Given that until the mid-1850s conflicts over slavery surfaced and then disappeared without being resolved, we are left with a question: Why, at this time, was there resort to warfare? Our finding supports Michael Morrison's: "Both sides were determined to live up to and live out their revolutionary heritage."[1] We also agree with Susan-Mary Grant's conclusion that northerners identified their society as the epitome of "the true republic" and were convinced that southern society was antithetical to that republic.[2] We found, as Jonathan Adkins did, that "for so long republican ideology had convinced them [southerners] that policies involved a constant struggle to defend freedom against scheming *conspiratorial* demagogues."[3] Moreover, we concur with James McPherson: Americans of both the North and the South believed themselves to be custodians of the legacy of 1776.[4]

Our reading of newspapers provides additional evidence to support their theses. It suggests that the slavery-republic link may be even more important and complex than has been recognized, and it raises, although it cannot answer, another question, in what ways did the presence of mass media influence the course of events?

ACKNOWLEDGMENTS

Many scholars have searched for an answer to the question of why, after more than a half-century of nation-building, the Union dissolved. Our debts to them are evident in our text and notes. So, too, is our debt to those who have wrestled with questions about the impact of newspapers' rise and transformation into mass media and about the role of such media in a democratic society. We have come to grips with both questions, and our reading of the two, largely discrete, bodies of literature left us the task of connecting them. Our greatest debt is to these scholars.

More specifically, we thank Edward Caudill and Kelly Leiter of the University of Tennessee and Tom Hill of Oak Ridge, Tennessee, for reading portions of the manuscript and offering helpful suggestions. We also thank the librarians of the University of Tennessee, Knoxville, for locating boxes and boxes of microfilm for us and calling our attention to sources available electronically. In addition, we are grateful to Leanne Garland of the Abraham Lincoln Museum, Harrogate, Tennessee, for helping us locate Cassius Marcellus Clay materials. Her help may be reflected even more in a subsequent research project.

We thank Willis Regier, director of the University of Illinois Press, for his interest in the project and his support for it, and the readers commissioned by the Press for their suggestions for improving our manuscript. We heeded their advice. We also thank Mary Giles for editing that improved readability and caught errors.

Finally, we are grateful to our spouses for critiquing multiple drafts and for suggestions about editing. We dedicate this book to them.

Fanatics and Fire-eaters

INTRODUCTION

*We are not enemies, but friends. We must not be enemies. Though passion
may have strained, it must not break, our bonds of affection. The mystic
chords of memory, stretching from every battlefield and patriot grave to every
living heart and hearthstone all over this broad land, will yet swell the chorus
of the Union when again touched, as surely they will be, by the better angels of
our nature.*

In these concluding sentences of his first inaugural address in March 1861,
Abraham Lincoln expressed fear for his country's future and urged fellow citizens to remember its past. He was reminding Americans that the Union was the
product of their forebears' struggle to win freedom and to form a national government, based upon republican principles, and to protect that freedom. But
when the president was inaugurated, eight states already had seceded from the
Union. The implication of that action, as Lincoln addressed it, was that those
Americans seemed no longer to hear the "mystic chords of memory."[1]

Earlier in his speech Lincoln made clear what threatened the Republic. He
insisted that "one section of the country believes slavery is right and ought
to be extended, while the other believes it is wrong and ought not to be extended. This is the only substantial dispute."[2] But the question Lincoln did not
address in his speech, the next logical question to ask, was, Why did the break
come? Disunion came after long years of disagreement about the practice of
slavery and after numerous occasions on which Americans found ways to set
aside their differences on that subject for the sake of trying to create or to preserve a unified nation. This time, efforts to compromise failed. Why had the
public mood become so bellicose, and why was conflict among segments of
American society so intense that voices of anger, suspicion, hatred, and fear
drowned out those of moderation?

Efforts to construct a useful answer to that question need to start with a review of how and why newspapers were able to grow from "in-group" reading
matter for political and financial elites into real mass media. True, newspapers
were passed from hand to hand and were staples of conversation in taverns and
coffee houses, but a press did not exist for the masses through much of the first
half of the nineteenth century. By 1850, however, newspapers—thanks to rapid population growth and urbanization, to revolutions in printing and trans-

portation and to a growing reliance on the "magnetic telegraph"—could deliver news and commentary quickly. The first chapter of this book is devoted to outlining some historical developments that changed the press into a mass medium and the changes that resulted in how newspapers reported news, interpreted it for readers, and provided a forum so millions of people could learn about and participate in political debate.

By the 1850s, thanks to railroads and faster printing technologies, newspapers reached almost everyone. Telegraph information—often incomplete first impressions written and transmitted in haste for competitive reasons—flowed faster, feeding public hunger for news and political comment. Newspapers were the primary source of information about what happened in the world beyond each citizen's realm of experience, and the explanations they provided about events in that larger world were important. Newspaper editors and reporters influenced public opinion through subject matter choices and wording and by the images they evoked, doing much as well to shape the tone of public discourse. Between 1856 and 1861, the pages of those newspapers were filled with emotion-laden epithets such as "barbarians," "traitors," "mean-spirited," "cowardly," "unprincipled," and "conspiratorial."

Through the pages of the newspapers they read, Americans had daily or weekly encounters with other countrymen and other points of view. In the late 1850s, such strangers more often than not were portrayed as evil people who performed evil deeds. Such portrayals both contributed to and reflected the division of the American community that Lincoln addressed. As the new president said, slavery "was the only substantial dispute" touching off the conflict among Americans. It was an issue to which newspapers devoted much space, painting dark pictures of those with whom they disagreed. But the national debate over slavery was placed in the context of loyalty to republican principles.

Although this study describes how, beginning in 1856, the debate in which the questions of the culture of slavery and the preservation of the Republic merged, arguments that so divided Americans must be put into general historical context.

From the time of the American Revolution, the paradox of slavery existing in a society dedicated to freedom troubled at least some of the people some of the time. In different ways and to differing degrees, Washington, Jefferson, and Madison—all slaveholders—were troubled by the existence of slavery in America. Nevertheless, as men of state attempting to create a sense of unity among a divided people and working for the preservation of a fragile republic, each sought to skirt the issues involved and soften differences of feeling and interest among their people.

When in 1817 the American Colonization Society was organized with the avowed objectives of gradually ending slavery by purchasing slaves from their masters and then resettling those former slaves in Africa, both Jefferson and Madison endorsed the effort, as did a significant number of Americans from all parts of the country. The Colonization Society agenda was to fail for many reasons, however, among them the economic changes that created an even greater demand in the South for slave labor. Furthermore, few already-freed slaves showed an inclination to be resettled in a place that was foreign to them.

Just two years after the founding of the American Colonization Society, Congress became embroiled in debates about the status of slavery in territories ready to apply for statehood. In 1820 the Missouri Compromise balanced admitting Maine as a free state against admitting Missouri as a slave state. Further, slavery was to be illegal in the lands of the Louisiana Purchase north of 36° 30'. Once again, political leaders had stepped back from confronting the slavery-republic paradox. In the longer run, however, the implications of that paradox, the potential for conflict as the result of it, could not be sublimated.

In 1831 William Lloyd Garrison, a journalist and former supporter of the Colonization Society, began to publish a newspaper in Boston, *The Liberator*. Abolition of slavery was foremost among the reforms to which Garrison devoted his newspaper and his efforts. Throughout the 1830s, he and other like-thinkers published newspapers, wrote tracts, and made speeches in the hope of forcing resolution of the slavery-republic paradox by eliminating slavery. But these reformers were in a minority, and many persons, north and south, lashed out against them. Abolitionists were subject to mob violence and other outrages, including official interference with the mail, all aimed at silencing the reformers. Of course, such events dramatized even more the conflict between holding dear those freedoms the Republic was supposed to protect and accepting the presence of slavery in American society. If in the 1830s few advocated ending slavery, the abolitionists' messages—and the messengers themselves—were widely seen as threats to the Republic's security. Figuratively, and in a few cases literally, abolitionists became martyrs to the cause of free speech and press.

Throughout the 1840s Americans were caught up in the excitement of territorial expansion. In 1844, after years of debate, Texas was annexed into the Union. In 1846 the United States went to war with Mexico, and in 1848 the end of the Mexican War resulted in another acquisition of massive amounts of land. Much of that territory, as in the case of Texas, lay south of the Missouri Compromise line of demarcation, meaning that slavery would be legal in the new lands. Debate over slavery in newly minted states resurfaced, occupying an enormous amount of congressional attention for two years until a compromise was reached in 1850. That compromise, however, contained provisions that before long would again focus both public and political attention on the slavery-republic paradox.

As part of the new compromise, some northern legislators joined southern colleagues in supporting a fugitive slave act. As demand for slave labor grew and the corresponding market value of slaves increased, slave owners sought new means to capture runaways. The Fugitive Slave Act allowed them or their agents to identify, capture, and return to their place of origin anyone suspected of being a runaway slave. Whether in fact the person captured was a runaway would be decided in that place of origin. On a number of occasions, escapees from slavery, and sometimes lawfully freed slaves, were seized in the North and taken south. In a few instances, opponents of slavery sought to prevent those seizures, even by use of force. Such episodes, and the heated reports of them in the press, provided added examples of republican principles being violated in the process of protecting slavery. Both sides saw that there were such violations. Southerners believed that northerners, in violation of law, were denying them their property rights. Northerners believed southerners, in their search for runaway slaves, were trampling on the legal rights of northern states and their people.

By 1854, in a further effort to dampen the flash-point of the slavery-republic conflict generated by adding new states to the Union, Congress passed the Kansas-Nebraska Act. In this effort to push aside the American paradox, geographical demarcation was dropped; in its place, a concept labeled "popular sovereignty" was adopted. In effect, the people of a territory, in determining who would represent them in a convention to draft a constitution for a new state, would decide if slavery would be legal in that state. From the time of its adoption, the act exacerbated rather than settled conflicts over slavery. It also focused attention on other aspects of the slavery-republic paradox. The Kansas-Nebraska Act evoked controversies over law-making, obedience to law, and more. As with the other conflicts mentioned here, the focus of debate was the ability of republican institutions and societal values to coexist with slavery. That concern, far more than a concern over the slave-slaveholder relationship, was the source of the conflict. Study of the rise of newspapers as mass media shows that the issue of a republican society under law was paramount. Our focus in this book is on the dramatic accounts and commentary that appeared in American newspapers as they wrote about the series of events chosen for study here.

Our review of newspaper coverage of events leading to war begins with the Brooks-Sumner caning incident rather than earlier clashes. Although long-standing social, political, and economic issues provoked divisions between and among northerners and southerners, to understand why war came requires delving less into those conflicts and more into emotional turmoil generated by clashing issues. Those issues burned even brighter as newspapers used a rhetoric replete with anger, suspicion, and fear. The news reports of the actions we chose for study came within five years of the start of the war, in rapid enough succession to cause political firestorms, one on another, emotional conflagrations in the hearts and minds of people both north and south.

1   The Emergence of a Democratic Press

The years from the election of Andrew Jackson in 1828 to the start of the American Civil War in 1861 saw extraordinary changes in all aspects of American life. Not long before, in 1803, the Louisiana Purchase added more than eight hundred thousand square miles of territory, doubling the land controlled by the United States. Much of this land-wealth, however, was inaccessible until steamboats, canals, and then railroads allowed Americans to begin to solve the riddle of how to explore the vastness of their nation.[1] In effect, this transportation revolution helped change what seemed to some a negative in the form of too few people dispersed over vast spaces into a positive—more than enough land for a burgeoning population. Transportation advances provided people who made their livings in the 830,000 square miles provided by the Louisiana Purchase with vast potential markets for all sorts of goods.

Rapid growth in population and changes in where people lived and how they earned their livings brought both opportunity and difficulty. This booming society was a world of ups and downs, opportunities and disappointments, a world fluid enough to allow winners to become losers and losers to become winners.

The history of American newspapers in the three decades after the election of Andrew Jackson also provides dramatic evidence of how the nation was changing. When Jackson took office, newspapers generally were sold by subscription to a relative handful of men interested in government and politics or looking to newspapers for commercial information. By the time Abraham Lincoln was elected president in 1860, the major newspapers had changed from relatively expensive, small-output products of printing shops into cash-and-carry commodities that were cheap, readily available, and widely read in America's ever-growing urban centers, smaller cities, and towns. In roughly thirty years the newspaper business underwent a revolution equivalent to and making use of the transportation revolution.

By 1856, the year that begins this book's narrative of events preceding the Civil War, leading newspapers had been propelled into a new era by a technological revolution, which for the first time made American newspapers into truly mass media, with the power that term now implies. Newspapers came to be read widely, both in places of publication and, thanks to the railroads, farther away. Because of the telegraph, they carried news of events that could be, more nearly than ever before, described at almost the time they happened.

In larger cities—and even in mid-sized cities—competition among newspapers was intense. No longer did publishers wait for news and comment to come to them, passively clipping and pasting and printing news lifted from exchange newspapers. By the 1830s, reporting—the active gathering of news—began to be a trade, and reporters, editors, and publishers strove to present news that would interest, entertain, excite, and please a mass audience. Catering to readers' tastes as well as to their prejudices and opinions made newspapers a vital force, both shaping and reflecting the attitudes of the reading audience.

By 1850 the three characteristics of modern mass media were in place and accelerating: availability of steam-driven presses for reproduction, growing railroad networks for distribution, and rapid development of near-instantaneous communication via telegraph lines for gathering and disseminating the most important news. Together they added up to newspapers that had more outreach and the power to portray—and distort—events and to amplify, often exacerbate, political arguments.

Dramatic growth in population and even more startling growth in the number and competitive zeal of leading newspapers meant more readers as well as more competition for those readers. The development of high-speed presses meant that it was feasible for two circulation leaders among major big-city daily newspapers—which also offered weekly editions to outlying areas—to reach and influence many people. By 1850 all these changes and more multiplied business opportunities of American newspapers, transformed a trade into a burgeoning industry, and revolutionized communication in American society. For the first time the public was exposed to, benefited from, and was victimized by mass media. Circulations and power grew accordingly. The largest newspapers became exemplars of an innovative major industry because of their new-found ability to sell large numbers of newspapers and thus attract substantial advertising revenue.

By the time of the Civil War, three decades of innovations, some incremental, some startling in uses of new technology, changed American newspapers forever. Some big-city newspapers became veritable manufacturers; news was their commodity.[2] Most, of course, were not major forces commercially, either in news or commentary, on either the national scene or regionally. A small minority of urban newspapers had the greatest political, social, and economic impacts. Dailies clustered heavily in major cities, and both their numbers and circulations grew mightily during the last two antebellum decades. By the late 1850s a dozen daily newspapers were published in Philadelphia, ten in Cincinnati and St. Louis, and eleven in Chicago.[3] The great growth in competition—including newspapers costing a penny or two pennies—ushered in a time of sensationalism in some circulation-leading urban dailies and no doubt had a democratizing effect on readership, putting the working classes more and more into the habit of reading "the news."[4]

Circulations soared far faster than population growth. In 1840 a nation with a population of 17,069,000 was served by 1,404 newspapers, of which only 138 were dailies. By 1860 the nation's population had increased by 84 percent, to 31,443,000, but the number of newspapers had increased by 265 percent, to 3,725. The number of dailies reached 387, an increase of 276 percent.[5] In 1840 the annual circulation of newspapers (from known circulations) was just under 186.5 million (10.9 copies per capita annually). By 1860 newspapers' annual circulation reached nearly 888 million copies (28.2 copies per capita annually).[6]

The boom in circulation required more than an increase in population. It also relied on the invention of the steam-powered press. When Benjamin H. Day began the New York *Sun* ("It Shines for All") in September 1833, he had one compositor and a youth to help print perhaps a thousand copies of the small ($7^5/8$ by $10^1/4$ inches) four-page publication. Printing was laborious; the *Sun* could not have been printed at a rate of more than 250 sheets an hour, on one side and then on the other.[7] By 1837 the *Public Ledger,* a Philadelphia penny paper, was using a Napier press "propelled by steam" and capable of printing three thousand sheets an hour.[8] A decade later, that same newspaper was using a Hoe Rotary Lightning Press, which could turn out five to ten thousand copies of a four-page newspaper in an hour. (In a remarkable moment in 1837, rotary press inventor Richard Hoe witnessed some of Samuel F. B. Morse's early experiments with telegraphy at New York University. Once the telegraph was used successfully in 1844, Hoe directed his efforts toward creating a rapid press that could deal with the coming communication revolution.)[9]

By 1850 newspapers in major cities outside New York had adopted the Hoe press. This remarkably expanded printing capacity meant that big cities had a larger share of newspaper circulation than smaller cities. Allan Pred has noted that twelve of the twenty-nine major cities he studied for *Urban Growth and City Systems in the United States, 1840–1860* "were together responsible for about 60 percent of the total 1850 circulation, or eight times more than would be expected as a combined share of the nation's population."[10]

In just a few years, big-city newspapering became big business, with increasing needs for capitalization, expensive equipment, and skilled labor. In the 1830s, a printer could start a small-town newspaper if he could scrape together $500.[11] Even in New York City in 1835—then a city of roughly three hundred thousand—James Gordon Bennett, with only $500 in capital and a basement "office" consisting of planks placed atop packing crates, founded the New York *Herald.* Costs of founding a newspaper escalated rapidly. Editor Charles A. Dana of the New York *Sun* said that starting a daily in New York City in 1840 would have cost between $5,000 and $10,000, but the amount was as much as $100,000 by 1850.[12] That meant that large metropolitan newspapers needed extensive capital and dependable cash flow and operating income; governmental patronage no longer was sufficient. Advertising and circulation revenue became more reliable sources of funding in a growing, mass-market economy. Market economics, involving pleasing a broader spectrum of readers instead of trying to please ever-shifting party organizations or political supporters who might or might not pay their subscriptions, were a critical factor in commercializing the press.

Particularly in the two decades before the Civil War, the meaning of news changed. As Gerald Baldasty has observed, until then "editors had been relatively passive in news gathering, producing political essays and extracting political news from exchange newspapers."[13] In the decades before the Civil War, news ceased to be whatever accounts came to hand and came to mean "news is what's new." In competitive terms, it might have been expressed as "my news is newer than your news." Moreover, the news was not given in what modern readers might regard as that elusive and illusive quality "objectivity." News and commentary, taken together, gave newspapers qualities that attracted some readers but not others. By early 1858, when editor James Gordon Bennett was claiming a circulation of a hundred thousand a day for his New York *Herald,* he saw it as "'about the only Northern journal that has unfailingly vindicated the constitutional rights of the South.'"[14] The Springfield *Republican*'s Samuel Bowles agreed with Bennett's assessment. "'It is amusing,'" he wrote, "'to see the greed with which the *Herald* is snatched up and devoured on its earliest arrival here in the evening, and what is worse, to see the simplicity of these Southern fellows who seem to pin their whole faith upon it. Where Northern men look at it only for amusement, as they look at *Punch* or *Frank Leslie* [*Leslie's Illustrated Magazine*], Southern men swallow it gravely with a sign and a knowing shake of the head.'"[15]

In larger cities, rapid change was driven by competition for circulation. The race to get more news faster took larger staff sizes; no longer could scissors-and-paste copies from other publications by themselves make for a competitive newspaper. Alfred McClung Lee reported that by 1845 Bennett's *Herald* employed thirteen newshands—editors and reporters—plus twenty compositors and sixteen pressmen. Weekly expenses ran between $1,400 and $1,600. In the 1850s Horace Greeley's New York *Tribune* had 130 employees as well as out-of-town "special correspondents."[16] By 1853 the newspaper circulated more than fifteen thousand copies; the *Weekly Tribune*'s circulation had grown from fifty-one thousand in 1853 to more than two hundred thousand by 1860, circulating Greeley's antislavery views while entertaining readers with human-interest stories. Greeley also identified staff writers, urging them to sign their articles. This mid-1850s innovation was noteworthy because bylines were not common in newspapers until military commanders north and south required them once the Civil War was underway, the better to keep track of military correspondents and threaten them if they criticized a general or revealed information of use to the enemy.

Before the telegraph, transportation, especially transporting the mail, was communication. Whatever the means by which newspapers, magazines, and letters traveled, the mails remained of great importance during the 1850s. Thanks to federal policies and statutory support for free exchanges between newspapers dating back to the eighteenth century, the influence of newspapers extended far and wide.[17] Merrill Jensen's observation about eighteenth-century American newspapers borrowing from each other was true throughout the nineteenth century: "Editors . . . made constant use of the scissors so that the same news item or political essay often appears in newspapers all the way from New Hampshire to Georgia, sometimes with acknowledgment and sometimes not."[18]

Even after the appearance of the telegraph, the mail mattered a great deal in moving information. "In short," Richard Kielbowicz has written, "the post office and the press *together* constituted the most important mechanism for the dissemination of public information until the Civil War."[19] Furthermore, printed material in the two decades before the war made up the majority of the weight of material sent through the mail. Newspapers' dependence on the mail and supportive laws and policies promulgated by both Congress and the post office is difficult to overemphasize. Not only were there massive free exchanges of newspapers among editors, but there was also free delivery in counties of publication and the ability to mail publications at minimal postage rates.[20]

In some degree these policies favoring newspapers pushed them far beyond local impact, making some large-city dailies newspapers for the continent. The most sizable example was Greeley's New York *Tribune,* which was said to have a daily circulation of eleven thousand in 1847 but a weekly edition circulation—with newspapers sent great distances to subscribers—of fifteen thousand. By 1860 the New York *Weekly Tribune*'s circulation—reprinting articles from the daily—reached two hundred thousand, which made it the world's most widely circulated newspaper.[21] The Boston *Evening Transcript* also published widely circulated weekly and semiweekly editions aimed at readers in smaller cities or towns and rural areas. The largest city-area daily newspaper circulation in the United States evidently belonged to the flamboyant James Gordon Bennett's highly criticized but widely read New York *Herald.* Even his most caustic critics had to give that devil Bennett his due. An observant contemporary, Lambert A. Wilmer, wrote in 1859 that Bennett's newspaper was "read by people of all classes, and its power and influence are universally acknowledged. Although the *Herald* is denounced from one end of the country to the other as the most corrupt and profligate in existence, its opinions on almost every subject are often quoted as indisputable authority, and hundreds of other newspapers adopt its views and republish its statements without the least reservation."[22]

James Ford Rhodes called Greeley's *Weekly Tribune* the "'greatest single journalistic influence," with 112,000 subscribers in 1854 and many more readers. For Rhodes, its "readers were of the thorough kind, reading all the news, all the printed speeches and addresses, and all the editorials, and pondering as they read. The questions were discussed in their family circles and with their neighbors. . . . There being few popular magazines during this decade, the weekly newspaper, in some degree, took their place; and, through this medium, Greeley and his able co-adjutors spoke to the people of New York and of the West, where New England ideas predominated, with a power never before or since known in this country.'"[23]

Circulation relied increasingly on the postal service, which was a complex operation in the decade before the Civil War. The postal service attempted to serve hamlets as well as big cities, using whatever means of transportation that was fast, relatively inexpensive, and reliable. Until the telegraph reached California in 1861, steamships, stagecoaches, and, for a time, even the legendary pony expresses moved news across the continent, although the pony express, for reasons of bulk and weight, usually did not carry complete newspapers but rather half-ounce slips that were digests of telegraphic news.[24] Private, for-profit mail or shipping services also sprang up as entrepreneurs saw opportunities.

During the 1830s, stagecoach lines worked hard to accommodate mail volume but were overwhelmed by various items—including many newspapers—sent along many routes. The men who ran the railroads were primarily concerned with passengers and freight and relatively indifferent to carrying the mail. As Kielbowicz pointed out, railroads carried only 1 percent of the mail in 1835, although that grew to 16 percent by 1843. In 1838 Congress had prepared for a future that would escalate demands on the mail by deciding that all railroad lines were also post roads. In 1838 newspapers made up three-quarters of the weight of the daily mail sent out of New York City, and Postmaster General Amos Kendall declared, "'Indeed, but for the redeeming power of the railroads, it would become necessary . . . to give up the hope of transmitting letters and newspapers with the same speed.'"[25]

Furthermore, public policy as set by Congress decidedly favored circulation over wide areas by large and wealthy newspapers in major cities. The Postal Act of 1852, for example, allowed newspapers to reduce mailing rates by 50 percent if they paid in advance. That rule meant that far-away, big-city publications such as Greeley's *Tribune* could compete with, even undersell, the local newspapers of smaller cities.

In 1839 William F. Harnden began a precursor of what is now called an express company by carrying a satchel of letters and small packages between Boston and New York. That quickly changed to providing a railroad car between the two cities, which was staffed by agents who would protect valuables, including specie. Newspapers made use of this business to move news dispatches and drop off exchange issues for editors along the route.[26]

Mail service, particularly in the South, was less effective. Postal service there, even among major population centers, did not come close to equaling the service available between and among major cities in the North.[27] Moreover, the South had a relatively low number of miles of railroad track. Inspection of a map of railroad lines in 1850 shows perhaps a thousand miles of track in the South and perhaps five thousand miles in the North. Mobile, Alabama, for example, had no rail service. By 1860 the map of railroads in operation showed the Northeast and West—all the way to St. Louis, Chicago, Milwaukee, and beyond—as heavily cobwebbed with lines.[28]

It would appear that if the South had three thousand miles of track in 1860, with some evident disjunctions where railroad tracks had gaps, the North appeared to have well over fifteen thousand miles, logically connected commercial and informational arteries that geographically displayed some of the logistical disadvantages the South faced when it chose secession and war. Even so, despite more tenuous communication links, major newspapers of the South were mass media too. Their penchants for answering each others' versions of the news and editorial characterizations of issues, men, and events received full exercise, north and south.

Railroads accelerated the process of nationalizing the impact of leading New York newspapers. The Philadelphia *Inquirer* carried an expression of dismay about the spread of New York's biggest newspapers. It was said that the distribution network "literally carries New York over every railway, sets it down at every station, and extends it everywhere."[29] Editor Robert Barnwell Rhett of the Charleston *Mercury,* far from Newspaper Row in New York City, griped, "We have to go to New York papers for news of our own affairs."[30]

Speed in printing and delivery was complemented by speed in getting the news to the newspaper. The advent of the telegraph in 1844—and its meteoric growth thereafter—spurred and multiplied rapid changes. The process of turning news into a commercial commodity, already well underway with the clattering and chuffing of steam-driven presses and railroad distribution networks, accelerated even more rapidly with the telegraph. Developments in news flow after the telegraph are a paradigm for information dissemination throughout the twentieth century. Turning news into a marketable commodity did not necessarily increase its accuracy and did not encourage sober, reflective thinking. The Philadelphia *Morning Pennsylvanian* called the telegraph the curse of the nation, warning citizens to "'beware of this new power in our midst, more potent than "an army with banners." Its whole stock in trade consists in the perpetual excitement of the community—in a morbid appetite for startling news and a monomania for extravagant and almost incredible rumors.'"[31]

That dim view of the much-touted telegraph echoed words of warning from Henry David Thoreau, whose *Walden* first appeared in 1854: "We are in great haste to construct a magnetic telegraph from Maine to Texas; but Maine and Texas, it may be, have nothing to communicate. . . . We are eager to tunnel under the Atlantic and bring the old world some weeks nearer to the new; but perchance, the first news that will leak through into the broad, flapping American ear will be that the Princess Adelaide has the whooping cough."[32]

Despite Thoreau's dismissive hyperbole, Americans heard much more than the trivial via the telegraph. At the end of 1859, the Fredericksburg *Herald* carried an angry item laying blame for tensions between North and South: "'Newspapers and Telegraphs have ruined the country. Suppress both and the country could be saved now.'"[33] But that sour point of view amounted to spitting into the wind. Once the technology of the telegraph was available, its rapid spread was fueled by entrepreneurs eager to feed the growing demands of moving information in a fast-growing nation. The rise of manufacturing and of more rapid inter-regional shipping on railroad lines was hastened by the contemporaneous and interrelated development of the telegraph.[34]

On May 24, 1844, Samuel F. B. Morse tapped out a message from the old Supreme Court chamber in Washington, D.C., on his "magnetic telegraph" invention. The words "What hath God wrought?" were received and decoded by an assistant in Baltimore. Three days later, the New York *Sun* announced that the New York–Baltimore telegraph line was operable and then described something of the mechanics of constructing the lines and expressed a sense of wonder: "'The wire, perfectly secured against the weather by a covering of rope yarn and tar, is conducted on the top of posts about twenty feet high and one hundred yards apart. The nominations of the convention this day (Democratic national) are to be conveyed to Washington by this telegraph, where they will arrive in a few seconds. . . . At half past 11 A.M. the question being asked, what was the news at Washington, the answer was almost instantaneously returned: 'Van Buren Stock is rising.' This is indeed the annihilation of space.'"[35] That said, the telegraph at first was used primarily to move commercial information and only secondarily to speed news-gathering, but it was rapidly adopted to acquire what would be called "news breaks" during the twentieth century. Although Congress moved positively to try to serve the public interest by subsidizing and regulating the Post Office, the telegraph was allowed to grow with little government oversight.

Samuel F. B. Morse first demonstrated his magnetic telegraph in 1844, and in 1845 Amos Kendall became the first agent for three-quarters of Morse's patented invention. Kendall sought private investment to build four telegraph trunk wires following the main post and business routes. Within seven years, either Morse's licensees or their competitors—using other patents—had completed the trunk lines Kendall envisioned. The network of wires made use of the experimental line of 1844, which linked Baltimore to Washington, quickly extending that line to New York and Philadelphia. A second trunk line linked New York to Boston, and a third arced north and then west to Albany and Buffalo, to the developing Great Lakes cities and those of the Ohio and Mississippi valleys. The fourth extended the New York–Washington trunk on to New Orleans.[36]

The manic James Gordon Bennett, who raised exaggeration to an editorial art form, could not overstate the importance of the telegraph. In 1846, when Bennett's New York *Herald* was sharing private pony express information with the New Orleans *Crescent* (teaming up in order to get reports on the Mexican

War ahead of newspapers that relied on ordinary mail), he also used such telegraph lines as were available to speed dispatches to his office. He claimed that "'mere newspapers, the circulators of intelligence merely—must submit to destiny or go out of existence.'" Bennett's newspaper indeed spent great sums on the telegraph, publishing as much as ten columns of telegraphic news in one issue. The Boston *Evening Transcript* reported, perhaps a bit enviously, that those ten columns had included a message from New York's governor in addition to "'markets from various quarters, legislative proceedings, Mexican news, and Congressional proceedings including a long report of Mr. Calhoun's anti-war speech.'"[37]

The telegraph's competitive advantages made Bennett positively grandiloquent. He saw that the telegraph would make Washington newspapers less important in providing news of Congress and the national government:

> "By means of the telegraph the local advantages of the Washington papers are transferred to this metropolis, and the superior enterprise and pecuniary means of the journals here will enable them to turn these advantages to the best account. Next session of Congress, we mean to show what can be done in this respect. We will give telegraphic reports of congressional debates and proceedings which will defy competition, and fully satisfy the whole country. As for official or semi-official information to be obtained in Washington, we will be able to give it here, and diffuse it throughout the country, before the indolent papers in that remote village have printed it in their columns.

> "As matters stand there, no newspaper can exist in Washington without receiving the wages of corruption from Congress, in the shape of jobs and gratuities."[38]

The telegraph's growth was nothing short of astonishing. True, telegraph lines could be hung in a hurry. With no operational telegraph lines until 1844, wires connected most of the eastern, particularly the northeastern, regions of the nation by 1852, when seventeen thousand miles of telegraph wires were in use. By 1852 the telegraph—ahead of the railroads—had linked all of the nation's major population centers except San Francisco.[39] In addition, message demands quickly led to installation of multi-wire lines. There were fourteen wires between New York and Philadelphia, seven between New York and Buffalo, and seven linking New York to Baltimore and Washington, D.C. Two wires joined New York to the South's leading commercial center, New Orleans.[40]

The web of railroad and telegraph lines, far more complete in the North than in the South by the late 1850s, showed a divergence of cultures. The North was "communication rich," and the South was "communication poor." Once the Civil War began that became important for two reasons. First, the more

developed transportation-communication web in the North facilitated movement of both materiel and information needed to wage a war. Second, the
North's more complete communication network helped to maintain a more
effective community of ideas during the war.[41]

A now-familiar pattern was evident, superimposing new technology over
the old, with great flurries of entrepreneurial (and speculative) ventures. For-
tunes were to be made and lost. Unregulated competition led to reckless—
some thought suicidal—price-slashing by competing telegraph companies,
particularly involving multi-wire telegraph services that linked major cities.
This was true, Pred observes, "especially before the formation of the American Telegraph Company and the Western Union Telegraph Company in the
late 1850s."[42]

It did not take long for the marvel of the telegraph to change the way major
newspapers pursued and moved news. Early in 1846, less than two years after
Samuel F. B. Morse's successful transmission from Baltimore to Washington,
the New York *Herald* boasted of a "'Special Extraordinary and Exclusive Express'" train run between Boston and New York, *"the fastest express ever run in
the country. . . . The whole traveling time between the two cities, was seven hours and
five minutes, distance Two Hundred and Fifty miles.'"*[43] Impressive as the break-
neck speed of thirty-five miles an hour surely was, it could not compete with
the telegraph's near-instantaneous ability to flash messages from one city to
another.

Although American journalism history doubtless overemphasizes the history of East Coast newspapers in general and New York City journalism in particular, it is hard to overemphasize the stature of New York of the 1850s as the
nation's financial and publishing center.[44] An important key to this centrality
occupied a small, grimy building at the corner of Broad Street and Wall Street:
the New York City Associated Press. The AP was owned by New York City's
seven leading newspapers, the *Courier and Enquirer, Express, Herald, Journal of
Commerce, Sun, Times,* and *Tribune.*[45] Maury Klein has described the conver-
gence among New York newspapering, the telegraph, and wire service news.
News via telegraph "made the nation more dependent on New York for news
because the Associated Press dominated telegraph dispatches and the New York
City press controlled the Associated Press."[46]

Domination of this sort, however, did not necessarily mean danger to
public welfare. That danger came from individual editors' and journalists'
distortions of telegraphic dispatches and from placing and interpreting the
accounts into regional and political contexts. The Associated Press was not the
main problem. That problem arguably grew out of understandably unprofes-

sional, and too often unprincipled, editor-advocates who fed public passions in the pursuit of political ambition or personal gain.

The power of the AP belied its dingy quarters. It was connected by telegraph to bureaus in Albany and Washington and had several full-time reporters as well as fifty "agents" around the nation who looked in local newspapers for stories of regional or national interest. The metallic sputter of incoming and outgoing messages kept a battery of telegraphers and clerks busy. The noisy clatter symbolized a new age of centralized news-gathering and distribution, making news truly a commodity.[47] An upstate New York newspaper termed the New York Associated Press "the most potent engine for affecting public opinion the world ever saw."[48] The expensiveness of telegraphic transmission, coupled with the New York AP's wish to sell to newspapers, in time had a substantial effect on news copy. Under the aggressive leadership of its second general agent, Daniel Craig, the New York AP did its best to stamp out competition in cooperative news-gathering. By 1855, for example, the competing service, Abbott and Winans, was out of business.

By the 1850s, the major dailies—particularly those of New York City—had become modern mass media, swaggering new giants that pursued financial gain and political power and had little evident concern beyond self-serving goals. The technologies of information transmission, printing, and distributing newspapers via the mail, railroads, or express services converged and multiplied some publications' influence far beyond their proprietors' wildest imaginings. Table 1 considers the technological timeframe for changes among newspapers that played substantial roles in dividing the ironically named United States into two warring nations.

American ingenuity in transportation and communication—celebrated and praised in many books, including Thomas Kiernan's *The Road to Colossus: A Celebration of American Ingenuity* and Maury Klein's *The Flowering of the Third America: The Making of an Organizational Society, 1850–1920*—had a darker

Table 1

	1840	1850	1860
Number of four-page papers printed in one hour (steam-driven presses available in 1840; rotary presses in 1853)	4,000	12,000	20,000
Miles of telegraph lines in service	0	12,100	50,000
Miles of railroad lines in service	2,818	9,021	36,626

Sources: Data on miles of telegraph and railroad lines are from Allan Pred, *Urban Growth and City-Systems in the United States, 1840–1860* (Cambridge: Harvard University Press, 1968), 176, table A-1.

side.[49] Fissures in the life of the American Republic, held in check by custom and compromise and by the common values of North and South, were put under additional (and, it might be argued, intolerable) strain by tectonic shifts in newspaper circulation and content that rose to a crescendo during the 1850s.

Newspaper publishers and editors could and did shape public opinion because newspapers were the primary source for regular information about governance and political institutions in the United States, north and south. The extent of their influence has been and should be questioned, but there is no doubt that newspapers' depictions and views of events were critical to what readers thought. Newspapers inevitably and sometimes tragically helped citizens form a partial understanding of their world and also helped shape their enthusiasms and hatreds.

Newspapers often reinforced readers' traditional values and attitudes, encouraging them to retain faith in existing institutions and feel secure about the motives and skills of their societal leaders. Conversely, newspapers could tear down what defined and sustained a mid-nineteenth-century American community. Then as now, the press did not speak with one voice, and viewpoints and stridency varied.

The newspapers' words often were published with no sense of responsibility that would have provided readers with a full and fair view of what had happened and why. Newspapermen seldom portrayed key actors responsible for events with the fairness of merely reporting their words and deeds. In effect, the newspapermen of the 1850s functioned without rules that might have guided or restrained them and without evident understanding of the desperately high stakes involved as a war of words helped bring on a war of bullets. Their business operated without ethical standards, and the reading public and society in general paid a price for that lack. America's first mass media were driven in the 1850s by a hunger for profit and power—a distant, echoing predictor of the feral pursuit of profit by the merging communications conglomerates of the late-twentieth and early-twenty-first centuries.[50]

Technological advances meant that for the first time newspapers could reach a mass audience. The prospects and reality of a much larger reading public stirred a dramatic increase in the number of newspapers seeking to attract their shares—the larger the better, of course—of that audience. Transportation's increasing speed and lowered cost allowed a few major newspapers to find readers virtually nationwide, and the new competitive environment led to changes in newspaper content and style.

As late as the 1840s, many of America's newspapers were the creations or creatures of political parties and their leaders. Without support made available by government printing contracts, many would have had difficulty surviving financially. Thanks, however, to faster printing presses and emerging mass markets, by the 1850s editors worried less about pleasing politicians, and there are indications that politicians worried more about pleasing editors. Recognizing earlier than most the changes unfolding in the newspaper world, in 1845 James Gordon Bennett reveled in the prospects for a new journalism. "'That journalism,'" he declared, "'which possesses intellect, mind, and originality, will not suffer. Its sphere of action will be widened. It will, in fact, be more influential than ever. The public mind will be stimulated to greater activity by the rapid circulation of news. The swift communication of tidings of great events, will awake in the masses of the community a keener interest in public affairs. Thus the intellectual, philosophic and original journalist will have a greater, more excited and thoughtful audience than ever.'"[51]

By the 1850s, thanks to the telegraph and the railroad, editors at major daily newspapers no longer waited quietly to get and to distribute news of their cities and states, the nation, and the world. Big newspapers, turned suddenly into true mass media because of swift news-gathering, printing, and distribution, provided editors and publishers with unaccustomed power and prestige and could bring entrepreneurs wealth and widespread political influence. Editors, coming from a time when a circulation of four or five thousand would make for a healthy daily, saw circulations soar and their voices become amplified.

The enormous leap from a cottage industry requiring little investment to sizable, capital-intensive mechanized printing plants in the space of just a few years caught newspapers unprepared to deal with the daunting if unpredictable power they now held. Both pushing technology and pulled by it, the character of newspapers changed as competition increased for the newest news, often news happening hundreds or thousands of miles away. The hunger for news was fed by information from near and far; recent news and recent sensations became essential elements in building and keeping circulation.

The most prominent newspapers raked in advertising and circulation revenue great enough to be handsomely profitable. With the largest big-city dailies, the scale of operations changed so that reliance on printing contracts and other politically based support faded. (The *National Intelligencer,* a semi-official newspaper concentrating on reporting on congressional debates and actions, was for years a major exception.) In general, newspapers shifted to patronage of a different kind, the patronage of readers. Newspapers, however, clearly propelled by readers' interests, exhibited continuing fascination with politics and frequently battled on behalf of particular parties and their candidates. Some editors, in fact, sought—and some attained—elected or appointed political office.

In this period, handling news evolved into something closer to a modern model of newspaper operation. Increasingly, news was distinguished from overt editorial opinion on major newspapers, both north and south, during the 1850s, but the opinions characterized the facts presented in the news, coloring the way events were perceived. The growing separation of "news" columns from "editorial" columns did not mean that news automatically became balanced or even-handed. As sociologists say, news is a social construct. During the middle years of the nineteenth century, it became a financial construct as well, a "manufactured product . . . reflecting the financial requirements of the newspaper organization, the commercial vision of its producers, and the day-to-day exigencies of production."[52]

Increasingly, reporting became a trade, but one with only the most rudimentary notions of fairness or accuracy or objectivity. Hazel Dicken-Garcia, a leading scholar of nineteenth-century journalistic standards, has concluded that it is impossible to generalize about accuracy of newspapers of that era from the perspective of late-twentieth-century standards. From a contemporary point of view, she observes, it cannot be known what went unreported. Moreover, where politics were concerned, the ambitions of some of the most prominent editors—including those who dreamed of the presidency or had gained elective or appointive office—in effect guaranteed that political news would not be presented even-handedly. Furthermore, in the 1840s, when many important newspapers were largely political and partisan, funded by politicians, government officials, or their supporters, content tended to be one-sided even as newspapers shifted from political-partisan emphases to broader news content. "[A]ccuracy," maintains Dicken-Garcia, "is in any case irrelevant as a measure of content that was intended to argue political points of view—as was true of most content up to the Civil War."[53]

The mid-nineteenth-century lack of independence in political terms may be difficult to fathom now. Editors and publishers who lust after political office may still surface, but not as frequently and prominently as they did during the 1850s. During the presidency of Andrew Jackson, before technological developments allowed real mass production of many daily newspapers, a newspaper that was truly independent politically was a rarity and generally did not stay in business long. Even if newspapers had not been founded by a political party or supporters of an individual politician, they were often reliant on political subsidies in one form or another, whether the aforementioned printing contracts or patronage jobs for editors, to help ends meet. The careers of Horace Greeley of the New York *Daily Tribune* and Henry Raymond of the New York *Times* both exemplify the actions of men who vigorously, at various times, sought elective office.

In the South, consider the wild-writing Robert Barnwell Rhett, South Carolina editor-politician and, beginning in 1848, part owner of the Charleston *Mercury*. Both a fiery speaker and editorialist, the lawyer Rhett moved from politics to newspapering. Elected to the U.S. House of Representatives in 1826 at age twenty-five, Rhett resigned his House seat in 1832 for a four-year stint as his state's attorney general. Reelected to Congress in 1837, he then was elected in 1850 to the Senate for the remaining two years of George McDuffie's term. Rhett was disappointed when not chosen to chair the Confederate Provisional Congress organizing the Confederate States of America in 1860. Despite the fame he attracted from his perfervid editorials—he was frequently quoted in northern newspapers because of his extreme and pungently expressed views—the *Mercury* was overshadowed at home by rival papers in Charleston and lost money. Nationally, however, Rhett was often considered a prime spokesperson for the South, and his editorials were frequently reprinted. Editorializing on the election of Abraham Lincoln in November 1860, for example, a defiant and warlike Rhett editorial declared the central issue to be northern efforts to extinguish slavery: "'The Southern States are now in the crisis of their fate . . . nothing is needed for our deliverance but that the ball of revolution be set in motion.'"[54]

If conflict of interest was not an obvious concern, neither was the concept of serving the public's right to know. That phrase was not common coinage during the first half of the nineteenth century, although at times glimmerings of a philosophy of access to information about the doings of public officials and bodies so the public could protect itself could be found in the press.[55]

Journalists often claimed fairness and balance—that is, telling all sides of a story, or at least more than one—as a practice or at least as a goal. In practice, however, balanced coverage was more the exception than the rule, other than the muted opinions in Associated Press copy and the reporting of other cooperative news-gatherers who had to serve many masters.[56] At times, in an effort to avoid trouble, editors would print opinions that ran counter to their personal and editorial views. In times of real crisis, however, as the antislavery editor Elijah P. Lovejoy learned, even trying to provide competing views on hot issues could not furnish safety from the violence of true believers. Lovejoy and his newspaper were mobbed repeatedly, and he was eventually martyred in 1836 in Alton, Illinois, by a proslavery mob.

By the 1850s, however, the mainstream press had less to fear from government suppression or private lawsuits for defamation than in earlier years. Yet freedom for mainstream newspapers, even if they could get away with extremes of political vituperation, was a narrow freedom at best. The right to agree with the dominant views of a society is a poor substitute for freedom.

True, mainstream newspapers during the 1850s generally were free to print what they pleased, because their views generally did not carry them onto dangerous ground. Topics to beware of were pro-abolitionist sentiments in the South (and sometimes in the North). As pro-southern publisher Gerard Hallock of the New York *Journal of Commerce* found after the firing on Fort Sumter in 1861, it was unsafe for him to stay in newspaper work in the North. He retired. Beyond those key issues, newspaper editors generally were safe from mob attacks in the 1850s, although there had been sufficient examples of canings of editors or mobbings of newspapers in earlier days to keep journalists in a wary frame of mind. Then as now, they tended to avoid local flashpoint issues that could lead to confrontations in the street or a howling assemblage outside a newspaper office. The New York *Herald*'s pugnacious editor James Gordon Bennett was thrashed on the street in front of his wife by an unsuccessful political candidate, and a bomb—discovered before it exploded—was delivered to his office in 1852.[57]

Then as now, the law of defamation was a consideration. Antebellum newspaper editors and publishers did have to be concerned about libel suits, which sometimes were pursued in multiples in an effort to "reason" with an editor or even to put him out of business.[58] Both the criminal and civil law frameworks for political defamation were alive throughout the 1850s. Seditious libel was out of favor, and the monumental unfairness of the Federalists' politically disastrous Sedition Act of 1798 was very much a part of the nation's cultural memory. The Sedition Act, which made it a crime to criticize the president, Congress, or federal courts, was used successfully to prosecute fourteen Jeffersonians, including the editors of some of the nation's most important newspapers. The language of the First Amendment ("Congress shall make no law . . . abridging the freedom of speech, or of the press") was of little avail in the face of Federalists' fear and loathing of French revolutionary doctrine, which John Quincy Adams's supporters linked to Jefferson and his friends. Criticism of the Federalists was characterized as disloyalty to the nation and therefore expression to be silenced and punished. Even though the Sedition Act made truth a defense to libel charges, truth was irrelevant when Federalist judges presided over Federalist jurors who got to rule on whether hated political opinions were "false."[59]

The Sedition Act, which became a powerful political rallying cry against the Federalists and helped ensure the election of Thomas Jefferson as president in 1800, was allowed to expire in 1801. Even Jeffersonian Republicans, however, were unopposed to seditious libel in principle. Jefferson and others of his party advocated using state common-law sedition prosecutions to bring opposition newspapers to heel as long as they were not brought under a federal statute.[60] Although common-law prosecutions for sedition or criminal libel were still possible after 1800, the weapons of choice against rambunctious newspapers became civil defamation suits seeking monetary damages. In cases involving hot partisan struggle, editors could face multiple lawsuits.[61]

In the 1840s in general, political libel suits became less frequent, but the decrease seems to have been more the result of changing political culture rather than liberalization of libel laws. In most states, truth still was not a complete defense to a civil libel suit; a workable defense meant having to prove truth as well as good motives and justifiable ends for publishing. If a libelous statement was reprinted from another newspaper, the reprinting editor—generally in no position to check the facts underlying the report—could be held legally responsible. That was the rule in New York and in most other states as well.[62]

At the same time civil libel suits were diminishing as threats to newspapers, by the 1840s voices were heard praising the American press as central to a free system of government. The Ohio jurist Frederick Grimké's *Nature and Tendency of Free Institutions,* for example, advocated freedom of argument within a system of contending parties. Even abusive partisan publications, he argued, should be free to voice their extreme arguments. Grimké declared that political argumentation—even coarse and abusive language—was not harmful to the public weal; indeed, it helped citizens to understand issues and participate in government. This lawyer-philosopher's views were precursors of Justice Oliver Wendell Holmes's "marketplace of ideas" from the sedition cases of the World War I era. Grimké praised the effects of a press with "'so many opinions, causing light to be shed upon each'" that even efforts to widen divisions in society could have a healing influence. Even political lies could be valuable where there were contests of opinions and ideas in a framework that had little in the way of legal controls.[63]

Such liberty-loving straws in the winds of the nineteenth century were more than counterbalanced by continuing efforts to suppress antislavery arguments. In the South, hatred for the antislavery drive and apprehensions over a large captive population all tied in to fears driven by myth and memory associated with the Nat Turner slave rebellion of 1831. These were among the forces behind another form of sedition law, although it was not called sedition in the statute books. In Virginia, for example, beginning in 1832 a series of statutes was passed making it a crime to speak or write in favor of abolishing slavery or to publish arguments that slaves were not property. In the South, abolitionist literature was declared to be illegal and unfit for the mails.[64] In the North from the mid-1830s into the 1850s, anti-abolitionist agitation showed that true freedom for a person who had hated ideas was often tenuous. Violence against speakers and the press was and is a common occurrence in times of societal stress. As communication historian John C. Nerone observed, violence is "an integral part of the culture of public expression in America." After a long study of violence triggered by publishing or speaking he concluded, "Violent events are systemic rather than episodic responses to recurring crises in an evolving system of expression."[65]

From the 1830s through much of the 1840s, mob actions against the abolitionist press were common. Dislike for the outspokenly fiery William Lloyd Garrison, publisher of *The Liberator,* boiled over into outright hatred and mob violence in Boston in 1835. Garrison had offered to sponsor British abolitionist George Thompson for a speech to the Ladies Anti-Slavery Society. Handbills appeared offering a $100 reward for the first person to do violence to Thompson, and his speech was canceled. The mob, however, found Garrison hiding backstage in Faneuil Hall, put a rope around his neck, and walked him out to the street. He subsequently was rescued by constables and put in protective custody before leaving town for several weeks until passions cooled.[66]

To abolitionist publishers including James G. Birney of *The Philanthropist* of Cincinnati, the cause of abolition was identical to the cause of a free press. Birney said the slavery establishment in the South was claiming a "'peculiar favoritism to the Constitution . . . demanding, with lash in hand, of States sovereign as itself, that all *their rights* should bow in submission.'"[67] In line with a morally bankrupt pattern persisting throughout American journalism history, another Cincinnati editor, James F. Conover of the *Whig,* in effect declared that newspapers not in agreement with his views had no legal rights. Abolitionist papers, Conover declared, were "'licentious and demoralizing, and occupy a ground by no means entitling them to legal protection.'"[68] Many citizens of Cincinnati viewed antislavery agitation as dangerous in stirring up disaffection among slaves; moreover, it might damage the city's hopes for economic development. Abolitionists, it was asserted, could harm Cincinnati's trade with the southern states. By July 1836, mass meetings were being held, and a committee tried to talk Birney and the Ohio Anti-Slavery Society into suspending the *Philanthropist.* Publication continued, but on July 30 a mob smashed Birney's printing equipment and shoved his presses into the Ohio River.[69]

The murder of newspaper editor Elijah P. Lovejoy in August 1836 is perhaps the most famous example of anti-abolitionist violence against the press. Lovejoy, an ordained Presbyterian minister, had begun his St. Louis *Observer* late in 1833. He did not see himself as an abolitionist, but he did fight against the sins of intemperance, greed, Sabbath-breaking, and owning slaves. This devout man, who served as secretary of the Missouri Bible Society, did not get into harm's way until 1835. Then, it was reported from Jefferson City that a box of Bibles sent from the society's St. Louis office contained abolitionist tracts.

Attacks on Lovejoy in other St. Louis newspapers followed, with an editorial in the *Commercial Bulletin* saying that abolitionists were being watched and that "'their slightest movement will bring down on them a summary punishment. *They will be put down.'*"[70]

Lovejoy argued vainly against efforts "'to frown down the liberty of the press and forbid the expression of opinion,'" but his words did not persuade a mass meeting of the good citizens of St. Louis. To the anti-abolitionists, freedom of speech did not include a right to discuss slavery, "'a question too nearly allied to the vital interests of the slaveholding States to admit of public disputation.'"[71]

Lovejoy argued that the abolitionist literature had been included accidentally with the shipment of Bibles and added that no law forbade him from sending anything he wished to friends, despite mob actions in burning books and newspapers. Contending that he was an emancipationist and for the gradual freeing of slaves rather than an abolitionist wishing immediate manumission, Lovejoy argued bravely that one day's decree against discussing property could be the next day's decree forbidding speaking against drunkenness. "'The truth is, my fellow citizens, if you give ground a single inch, there is no stopping place.'" Therefore, Lovejoy declared, it was his duty to "'take my stand upon the Constitution.'"[72]

Such bravery quickly proved dangerous, especially when coupled with the *Observer*'s May 28, 1836, denunciation of the lynching of a black man, tied to a tree and burned to death, who had been arrested for murder. Lovejoy's newspaper also attacked as "papist" by the appropriately named Judge Luke E. Lawless. Judge Lawless instructed a grand jury that it need not indict members of the lynch mob; after all, their passions had been inflamed by a newspaper that abused liberty of the press.[73] Mobs repeatedly damaged Lovejoy's office, and his home was vandalized.

In June 1836 Lovejoy moved his newspaper about fifteen miles northeast and across the Mississippi River to Alton, a town in the free state of Illinois. His press, while sitting on a dock in Alton, was broken apart and thrown into the river by a mob. But Lovejoy persevered. Once he had a press operating again, his *Observer* became fervently abolitionist. Rival newspapers, including the *Missouri Republican* and the Alton *Spectator,* editorialized in favor of mobs and against the right of free expression for the unwelcome editor.

Lovejoy, meanwhile, was becoming a hero in other parts of the nation. A plea for funds netted him $1,500 needed for a new press—his third. As soon as it arrived, however, a mob destroyed it, too. In Kentucky, the Louisville *Gazette* and the Lexington *Intelligencer* expressed admiration for Lovejoy's courage. When a fourth press arrived on November 5, 1836, it was stored in a warehouse for safe-keeping. On November 7, hearing of an attempt to destroy the new press, Lovejoy went to the warehouse with armed supporters. When a mob appeared, shots were exchanged and one man was killed. The mob withdrew, soon returning with ladders to climb onto the roof to attempt to set fire to the structure. Lovejoy, standing in the doorway of the warehouse and holding a rifle, was killed when riddled with five bullets.[74]

To many newspapers in the North, including the New York *Evening Post* and Horace Greeley's *New-Yorker* (which he edited before the *Tribune*), Lovejoy was a martyr to the causes of antislavery and freedom of the press. A minority of newspapers in border states and Bennett's New York *Herald* saw his martyrdom as strengthening the cause of abolitionists.[75] As Lovejoy found, however, to be opposed to slavery—even when he was a gradualist, an "emancipationist"— could be dangerous to the point of death.

One who favored emancipation publicly and survived an assassin's knife was the legendary Cassius Marcellus Clay of Kentucky. In 1845 Clay, a cousin of the even more famous Sen. Henry Clay, began publishing a newspaper urging emancipation: the Lexington *True American*. Two thousand people gathered in Lexington to protest its publication. Ultimately, while Clay lay ill with typhoid fever, a mob entered his heavily armored printing house. The warlike Clay had lined his office walls with muskets and pikes and had placed a cannon loaded with bits of chain and nails just inside the front door, facing outward. While Clay was on his sickbed, what was described as a rather gentlemanly mob packed up the *True American*'s press and type and shipped them off to Cincinnati. Soon thereafter, Clay left Kentucky to fight heroically in the Mexican War, surviving months of captivity.

By 1849 Cassius Clay was a prominent figure in Kentucky's Liberal Party, a combination of slaveholding and non-slaveholding emancipationists. Speaking at Foxtown, only a mile from his White Hall mansion near Richmond, Kentucky, Clay was set upon by at least ten men and stabbed in the lung and breastbone with his own bowie knife by Cyrus Turner, son of a proslavery politician. Clay managed to wrest his knife away from Turner and stabbed him in the abdomen. Clay fainted, but not before crying out that he died in the defense of the liberties of the people. Turner, however, was the one who died. The fracas was widely reported, including in Greeley's New York *Tribune*.[76]

There were 134 instances of anti-abolitionist (or anti-emancipationist) violence between the late 1820s and 1861, according to a study by John C. Nerone. The majority of the violence was said to be against individual speakers, with only twenty-four instances directly involving the press. After the firing on Fort Sumter on April 12, 1861, however, there was an upsurge in violence in locations ranging from Beaver, Pennsylvania, to San Francisco, where mobs materialized at four newspapers. Mobs in New York and Brooklyn visited a total of eight newspapers, generally to enforce their "patriotism" by making sure the newspaper offices were flying the American flag.[77]

Flying the flag was a real necessity for Bennett's *Herald*, which had to back away from attacks on the Lincoln administration published just before Fort Sumter, vituperation calling for overthrow of a "vicious, imbecile, demoralized" government as the only chance to avoid war.[78] Threatened by a mob on April 14, the *Herald* whirligigged its stance overnight, publicly declaring itself to be pro-Union on April 15. By April 16 the *Herald* was organizing that wealthy newspaper's extensive system of war correspondents; eventually, there would be sixty-three. The pro-southern Gerard Hallock, editor of the New York *Journal of Commerce* and president of the New York Associated Press, was not as fortunate. Clearly fearing for his life, he resigned his AP post and retired from his newspaper.[79]

Extralegal forces thus could bring threats to be reckoned with. They included occasional reader-to-editor violence and boycotts called in New York City against Bennett's sensational *Herald* by less-sensational journals. Overall, however, litigation and extralegal threats did not discourage the most prominent editor-publishers. Their newspapers provide a window on a time when the words of the First Amendment were largely without content and, aside from occasional self-flattering encomiums, editors and publishers gave little attention to the responsibilities of the press.

The extent of freedom seemed to be dictated and defined by the people—by what they would tolerate at different times and in different places—and not by government. But with the major exception of the lingering stain of antiabolitionist violence, which had faded during the 1850s because few abolitionists north or south dared to speak out stridently, fear of mob action against the press became less compelling until the actual outbreak of hostilities at Fort Sumter. If a newspaper published messages that were within the area of public toleration if not sympathy, mobs did not materialize and boycotts were not organized.

Newspapers were in positions of power but had precious little sense of responsibility to society, a potentially disastrous combination in a nation where political compromise no longer could contain centrifugal issues and impulses. Publishers and editors, eager entrepreneurs, saw their role as publishing words to attract an audience in order to turn a profit and magnify their voices in support of political and social causes they favored. The First Amendment was little more than a historical reminder that the Revolutionary generation had a vaguely stated concern for preserving "the freedom of speech, or of the press." In operation, freedom of the press in the United States of the mid-1850s seemed to have two meanings: whatever editors and publishers thought they could get away with or whatever government or their public would tolerate, particularly in a time of crisis or when a topic was involved that roused readers' emotions.

The first American media barons began as scruffy tradesmen in major cities. The prototypical mass newspaper in New York was the product of Benjamin H. Day's struggling printing shop. Day, a former apprentice to the respected Samuel Bowles of the Springfield *Republican,* had moved on to New York, where he worked for three different newspapers in that city before opening his own job-printing business.[80] His printing house foundered, however. Day had exhausted his skimpy savings to go into a business dependent on other businesses when he was confronted with a financial panic and a cholera epidemic that claimed thirty-five thousand lives. With his business failing in 1833, Day began to publish the New York *Sun,* modeled after the English *Penny Magazine.*[81] The tiny, four-page sheet—$7^5/8$ by $10^1/4$ inches—sold for a penny in contrast to New York's existing six-cent papers.

Day started the *Sun* as a desperate, last-ditch effort to save his printing business, even though four penny-paper experiments had failed earlier in Boston and Philadelphia. If readers would not come to the *Sun,* then the *Sun* would go to them. Day adopted the "London plan" of circulation and sold newspapers to men and boys at a discount for hawking through the streets.[82]

One of the first reporters in America materialized in Day's printing house during the *Sun*'s first week. An out-of-work printer, George Wisner, asked $4 a week to report on police court sessions that began at 4 A.M. daily. Court sessions provided moralistic human-interest stories and short, pithy police items ridiculing the unfortunate. Wisner's reports were instantly popular and sold many newspapers. He was so successful, in fact, that he was given a half-interest in the *Sun* within six months. His accounts of police court actions were famously raffish:

POLICE OFFICE—(Saturday morning)
    John Turner, of 141 Washington street, was charged with exposing himself naked in the street. Committed.
    Charles Lynch, of 130 Washington street, was charged with committing an assault and battery on Mary Lynch. Mary forgave him, and he was discharged.
    John Murphy, from York, U.C., had no home—no money no clothes—and slept in the Park. Committed.
    William Riley, of 28 Norfolk street, was brought up for abusing his wife. Bound over to answer the charge at the [Court of] Sessions.[83]

Later in the same issue's police court column, the *Sun* published a correction, which showed that it did have some fear of legal or extralegal retribution:

"Timothy Donohue, who was committed to prison Thursday morning for drunkenness and abusing his wife, is not the same person who resides at 31 Vesey street of that name. On the contrary, Mr. D. of Vesey st. is a worthy citizen."[84]

Within three years, the size of the paper expanded to 14 by 20 inches. After publishing Richard Adams Locke's "Moon Hoax" stories claiming that the famed astronomer Sir John Herschell had discovered fantastic creatures, including bats with human features, living on the moon, the *Sun*'s daily circulation soared past nineteen thousand, greater than the *Times of London*'s seventeen thousand. The *Sun*'s pressrun took ten hours on a Napier press.[85]

At first it was doubtless a misnomer to call the *Sun* a newspaper. Its formula for attracting readers had little room for the standard fare of six-cent newspapers, for it consistently did not carry reports of Congress or the New York legislature, political speeches, and other predictable staples of full-sized papers. The *Sun*, however, quickly found its rhythm and devoted its first and fourth pages to advertisements and fictional narratives and verse. The second and third pages consisted of brief paragraphs on court of sessions actions and police court cases, regaling readers with brief accounts of local murders, crimes, accidents, and fires in addition to clippings of similar events from other newspapers. After six months' operation, the *Sun* declared: "'When we began The Sun, we were determined to conduct an independent paper. * * * With TRUTH for our motto we alike disregard libel suits of the house-breaker, and the money of the office-seeker. And whenever the villainous conduct of a man, or a body of men—(no matter to what they belong)—may deserve exposure—so sure as we hold with our hands the whip so sure will we "Lash the rascals naked through the world.""'[86]

What Day had discovered was the power of sensation to titillate the masses and a way to make money from it. Such financial success attracted imitation. The New York *York Transcript*—edited by Asa Greene—began publishing just six months after the *Sun*, on March 10, 1834, with this appraisal of New York City's fiercely competing newspapers:

> "There are eleven 'large and regularly established daily papers' in this city, and with the exception of the Courier and Enquirer, and perhaps, The Times, not one of them employs a reporter, or takes any other pains to obtain accurate and correct information—on the other hand, there are two small daily NEWS papers (ourselves and our contemporary), and those two employ four reporters, exclusively to obtain the earliest, fullest, and most correct intelligence of every local incident; and two of these latter arise at 3 in the morning, at which hour they attend the police courts . . . while others are obtaining correct information about the city."[87]

The following year another penny paper was started in New York. James Gordon Bennett's *Herald* was a financial success soon after being founded on a shoestring in 1835, thanks to a shrewd mixture of sensational stories spiced with sex and violence and stories giving detailed news of markets. The *Herald,* in fact, was one of the first newspapers to provide up-to-date stock prices. Bennett, well educated in his native Scotland, understood commerce and finance and wrote about such matters with clarity and verve, helping to attract respectable readers who also could be amused by the *Herald*'s sensational fare.[88] By 1845 Bennett claimed a circulation of roughly twelve thousand on week days and about seven thousand on Sundays, "'the largest aggregate circulation of any journal in the civilized world.'"[89]

It didn't happen overnight, but technology fueled a true revolution in news-gathering. Starting with the largest newspapers in the largest cities, the race to acquire that perishable commodity called news became faster and faster. Gerald Baldasty has it right: "Definitions of news changed during the middle decades of the [nineteenth] century and contributed to the spiraling costs of newspaper production."[90] Until the 1840s, for the most part, reporting was little known, and essays of political bloviation were standard fare. As Baldasty explains, "The only genuine reporting of news, at least by twentieth-century definitions, was stenographers' reporting of congressional or legislative proceedings. By midcentury, reporting on news events was increasingly common, and the number of reporters on staffs rose."[91]

The scandalmonger reporters haunting police stations for Day and Bennett were part of the seamier side of the accelerating race for news, and greatly prized news of Europe led to efforts to meet incoming ships and relay incoming dispatches, reflecting growing competitive zeal to be first with foreign financial or political news.

Leading daily newspapers prospered in response to free-market economics, with freedom for editors to support causes they favored or even to thumb their noses at political parties and politicians, as Bennett's *Herald* did from time to time.[92] The leading editors were also free, in a time with no well-developed ethic of conflict of interest, to pursue political ambitions, as Greeley of the New York *Tribune,* Raymond of the New York *Times,* and Robert Barnwell Rhett of South Carolina's Charleston *Mercury* chose to do.

Biographical snippets about famous editors do not provide a well-rounded picture of the press. Beyond Bennett's viciousness, Raymond's competing muses of journalistic decency and political ambition, and Greeley's well-intentioned and sometimes brilliantly articulated waffling, hundreds of editors of daily newspapers around the nation took news reports from wire services and by clipping exchange papers, often seemingly in search of the most divisive issues or the most inflammatory southern or northern rhetoric on issues of the day.

Newspapers, north and south, often borrowed each other's words and used them as springboards for discussion and disagreement. Hatred begot hatred, and even a conciliatory-sounding suggestion in the New York *Times* was read by the New Orleans *Bee* as a coded statement revealing the perversity of abolitionist fanatics of the North. At the start of July 1857, the *Bee* referred to "a recent article in the New York *Times* saying the North . . . is slowly and unwillingly admitting that the systems of society, North and South, are 'radically and absolutely dissimilar,'" irreconcilable and inevitably hostile to one another. As quoted in the *Bee,* the *Times* had declared, "The 'Slavery Question' is the gravest question which any existing nation is called upon to solve. Are we in a way to solve it? It calls upon the people whom it confronts for the utmost calmness, the utmost fairness, for perfect freedom of investigation, for mutual tolerance, and mutual forbearance."

Those seemingly innocuous words set off an editorial paroxysm in the *Bee.* The North had no right to discuss slavery, either with or without moderation. "The social system of the South is peculiar, to be sure," the *Bee* declared, "but it is substantially the same now as it was at the formation of the federal compact. It was recognized by the Constitution." The *Bee* concluded that when the North insisted on a right to discuss slavery, "it offers perpetual molestation to the South, becomes meddlesome and annoying."[93]

With technology turning some of America's newspapers into mass media, editors came to wield, more dramatically than ever, the power now associated with such media. Then, that power was exercised as if words had no consequences for harm. If there was a popular suspicion that a conspiracy was underway in some aspect of public affairs (and conspiracy theories ran rampant in antebellum America), then editors would reinforce that suspicion. If a politician took an unpopular stand contrary to the general opinions held by a newspaper's readership, newspapers would publish attacks—not on the stand but on the character of the person taking the stand.

Events taking place beyond the immediate experience of a newspaper's readers were often overdramatized. In the 1850s, long before home delivery stabilized circulations, sensationalized news truly did sell newspapers. A controversial action by a few persons would be generalized as evidence of the behavior of an entire community or region, and the account of it sold papers. On occasion, an editor would take other editors to task for their lack of restraint, their distortion of the news, and their false characterizations of political personalities or whole segments of society. Such recognition of the need for self-imposed social responsibility, however, was rare and had little discernible effect or appeal.

The press was a powerful weapon wielded by those whose prime interest was self-interest. The consequences of that self-serving approach in manipulating the streams of public intelligence, both north and south, are evident in the ways in which the press described and explained events that, taken together, helped set the stage for civil war. Fighting words in newspapers, including those famous epithets *fanatics* and *fire-eaters,* applied name-calling not merely to handfuls of radicals but to whole societies. Such words provided sparks and tinder for the coming conflagration.

2 Impeding Civilization: The Brooks-Sumner Incident

The Mexican War provided a powerful stimulus to Americans' sense of national identity, but—ironically—it brought to center stage the conflict over the place of slavery in a society founded upon and still resting on republican principles. The acquisition of a vast land mass available for settlement made reconciliation of the issue of whether and where slavery could be extended more urgent than ever. After two years of congressional debate, debate that threatened to splinter the two major political parties, a compromise was reached. As is often the case with compromises, however, advocates who held staunchly to their positions were dissatisfied and angry. When the long-time political leader Daniel Webster of Massachusetts called for all concerned to set aside sectional interests for the sake of national unity, for example, he was denounced by some in his home state. From both north and south, important and ambitious political leaders decried acts that, taken together, made up the Compromise of 1850. A year later and after months of debate, Charles Sumner, a member of the Free-Soil Party and a bitter critic of the compromise, was chosen by the Massachusetts legislature to represent his state in the U.S. Senate.

In 1854 the question of where slavery could be established resurfaced like a bad dream. Once again a compromise plan was put forward, and once again compromise produced conflict. In January of that year, Sen. Stephen Douglas, an Illinois Democrat, introduced legislation to organize what was known as the Nebraska country into the territories of Nebraska and Kansas. Douglas had a number of reasons for pushing such legislation in order to provide for orderly development of this vast region. Because the region was not part of the Mexican War cession it had not been part of the Compromise of 1850. It was part of the Louisiana Purchase lands. As such, these lands were north of the line of demarcation set in the Missouri Compromise of 1820 that would seem to have precluded slavery for either of the proposed new territories of Kansas and Nebraska. These territories, given their rapidly growing population, would soon be states.

Douglas knew that to get the votes needed to approve his legislation he would have to hold out at least the possibility that the Kansas Territory might allow slavery. To accomplish that, Douglas proposed that citizens of each territory should decide the slavery issue for themselves. Their decision would be made after each territory was organized and be part of the proposed state constitutions. Application for statehood required the writing of a constitution for each territory, and citizens were to be allowed to vote on whether their state would make slavery legal. It took until May, but Douglas won approval of his plan. The Missouri Compromise's geographical determination of whether a state would be slave or free had been abrogated.

Residents of the newly created Kansas Territory now had to contend, in addition to disputes over land claims that plagued all new territories, with the issue of slavery. Congressional action made Kansas a battleground over local disputes and an issue of national import as well. The conflicts were many and often bloody.

It was in the context of events in Kansas that on May 22, 1856, Senator Sumner delivered a lengthy oration in which he not only addressed events in Kansas but also went beyond those happenings to emphasize the slavery-republic paradox. That afternoon in 1856, Rep. Preston Brooks of South Carolina entered the U.S. Senate Chamber and waited for the session to end and for the gallery to empty. Brooks then walked to Sumner's desk and proceeded to beat him on the head and shoulders with a cane purchased for that purpose. For the next three years Sumner was absent from the Senate.[1]

When Brooks approached him, Sumner was busy franking copies of a lengthy speech in which he had addressed the current conflict over slavery in the Kansas Territory. Long convinced of the evil of slavery, Sumner had labeled his speech "The Crime against Kansas." Had the Massachusetts senator limited his words to reciting the evils of slavery and denouncing the violence in Kansas from the collision of proslavery and antislavery settlers in the territory, the speech probably would have been little noticed. It was not the first time that Sumner had used his considerable rhetorical powers to denounce slavery. His views of—and passion about—the subject had been well known ever since he gave his first Senate speech in 1852, some nine months after he took his seat in that chamber. At that time, he had spoken in support of a motion he made to repeal the Fugitive Slave Act, which had been enacted as part of the Compromise of 1850.[2] Notwithstanding the power and passion of his oratory, his motion was defeated, with only four senators voting aye. But that was in 1852. Sumner's 1856 speech reflected the heightened tension both in the Congress and among the public at large over questions involving the extension of slavery into the territories. What was special about Sumner's 1856 speech was not his argument but his style. He personalized the debate on slavery through a diatribe aimed at the character of slaveholders in general, with particular reference to slaveholders and those he considered to be their allies in the Senate.

After a speech Sumner made in 1854 on the subject of slavery, several of his fellow senators, including Andrew Butler of South Carolina, who sat next to him in the chamber and with whom he had developed a cordial social relationship, had rebuked him both publicly and privately. Then, Butler denounced Sumner as a "miscreant" and a "sneaking, sensuous, snake-like poltroon." The South Carolinian urged the Senate to expel Sumner because his denunciation of the Fugitive Slave Act included what Butler considered an irresponsible call for the public to ignore the law. To Butler, Sumner had rejected the rule of law, a clear violation of his oath of office. Although Sumner was not expelled, he would neither forgive nor forget Butler's verbal attack.[3]

The text of Sumner's 1856 "Crime against Kansas" speech was peppered with references, highly unflattering references, to Senator Butler, Senator Douglas of Illinois, and other prominent Democrats. In verbally attacking Butler, who was absent from Washington at the time the speech was delivered, Sumner included a denunciation of the senator's home state of South Carolina and its people, suggesting that from the time of the American Revolution they had shown themselves to be traitors to the Republic. Further, Sumner likened Butler to Don Quixote and declared Butler's mistress to be "the harlot slavery."[4] Expanding upon the Don Quixote theme, the Massachusetts senator depicted Douglas as Don Quixote's devoted servant Sancho Panza, ready at any time and in any way to serve his southern master. In the speech, Sumner showed determination not only to attack the slavery issue but also to denounce the character of slaveholders and those sympathetic to them. Debating issues was one thing; engaging in character assassination was quite another. Sumner, seeing himself as the party wronged, had fought back by using his most effective weapon, the power of his words, to defend his character and, by associating his enemies with slavery, to defile their reputations.

Although the Kansas disputes had been much discussed in the press, the Brooks-Sumner incident, the public beating of one public official by another, focused attention on the conflict in a different and more compelling way. In the pages of the nation's newspapers the two personalities became symbols for the collective characters of the people of their respective regions. They became personifications of good and evil. Who and what was good and who and what was evil was in the eye of the beholder. Whatever the view, the clash over the issue of extending slavery into the territories, and whether slavery as an institution was right or wrong, had been reduced to the simplest terms: to personalities and the violent conflict between them. The contest between people from different regions and with loyalties to different political parties, or holding different views as to the role of the federal government, moved to a less abstract realm. With that move the danger to the Republic became more palpable.

For the public, the question became whose side you were on, Brooks's or Sumner's? As described in Democratic newspapers, whether published in the North or South, Charles Sumner was a fanatic abolitionist, willing to impugn the character of both elected representatives and a whole society to serve his cause. As those newspapers described and analyzed the situation for readers, Sumner would bring anarchy and war to the country and destroy the precious national heritage that had been entrusted to this generation of Americans to protect. Like those who came before them, Americans of both the North and the South were ready to believe that anyone who would wreak that sort of havoc for the sake of the "nigger" had to be a fanatic.

At the same time, a different segment of the northern press saw Preston Brooks as a wild-eyed zealot, a member of the slave-power conspiracy made up of men they labeled "fire-eaters." To those persuaded of the existence of that conspiracy, Brooks's use of force against Sumner was a clear example of the barbaric, unrepublican, and arrogant behavior of slaveholders in general. These were men who grew up exercising the power to control totally the lives of other human beings, to beat them and even kill them with impunity. Readers of some northern newspapers were told that Brooks was but one of many slaveholders who would plot against the Republic for the sake of preserving that power over people, whether they were slave or free, black or white. He was said to be, in fact, the epitome of the southern slaveholder, as the "nigger beater" standing over the bleeding and helpless form of not a black man but a white man, Charles Sumner, while Brooks's fellow southerners stood by snickering, doing nothing to stop the assailant.[5] Further, those northerners read about how Brooks's constituents applauded him and his actions. He was presented with replicas of the cane he had shattered while using it as a weapon, and his constituents later reelected him to Congress. For northerners, that was evidence of the grip slaveholders had on all of southern society and the threat they posed to any man, black or white, who challenged them.

The Republican press presented these views and, along with the negative images of Brooks, painted positive images of Sumner. Those newspapers described Sumner as a brave advocate of liberty and preserver of the heritage of the Republic. In the sacred halls of Congress, Sumner had used the power of free speech to argue for what he believed to be right. Whatever those editors might have thought about slavery, they insisted that Sumner was the champion of republican principles. He was described as the defender of freedom of speech and the victim of a foul conspiracy on the part of men whose lack of character and virtue was revealed so clearly in the dishonorable attack. He was beaten when he could not defend himself. Sumner was declared the epitome of a civilized person, and only civilized people could make a republic succeed. In contrast, Brooks was the epitome of depravity and barbarism. Men of such evil character would destroy the Republic.

On the southern side, Brooks was described as the defender of civilization. It was Sumner who was the barbarian whose behavior threatened it. Southern newspapers insisted that Sumner had defamed not only his fellow senators but also all other southerners. In their eyes, Brooks had taken on the "mad-dog fanatic" who threatened southerners' well-being. He had silenced him, and thus he was the hero.

Thanks to the telegraph and to the rapid exchange of newspapers, it took only a day or two for the press to spread word of the attack to all parts of the country. The public quickly knew that a South Carolina Congressman named Brooks had "punished," "beaten," "thrashed," or "tried to murder" Senator Sumner. The operative verb differed from newspaper to newspaper, and the difference, of course, immediately colored the reader's view of what happened and why. The "object" or the "victim" was either beaten senseless or whipped like a dog, depending on the account one read. Sumner was either close to death or had been helped up and walked out, chastened by the beating. He either cried out in pain and anger or "bellowed like a calf" as a coward would.

The press lost no time in proceeding from a description of what had happened to characterizations of why it happened. One day after the incident, in its May 23 issue, the *National Daily Intelligencer* of Washington, D.C., which devoted most of its news space to accounts of congressional debate and actions, took note of the incident by mildly characterizing it as a "painful occurrence." The incident, it said, was a "personal matter" that grew out of "personal provocation."[6] In the days and weeks that followed, the *Intelligencer* took no further notice of the attack. Neither did it assess it or offer more speculation about why it happened and comment on the post-incident furor to which other newspapers gave so much attention. Perhaps the reason for so thoroughly downplaying the incident was suggested in the newspaper's nameplate, which read "Liberty and Union, now and forever, one and inseparable." The Brooks-Sumner incident promised only trouble for those who put liberty and union above all else. At a less noble and more crudely self-interested level, taking a position on such a divisive issue could jeopardize the future of a newspaper that relied heavily on government printing to show a profit.

Other newspapers saw it much differently. Two days after the attack, the widely read New York *Tribune* declared that the caning was an illustration of "the poisons southerners spread."[7] The *Tribune* used the incident as evidence of how the North had shown "weakness and cowardice in the face of the South." After defending Sumner as a champion of freedom and a protector of the republican tradition of the Revolutionary heritage in an age in which self-seekers debased both, the *Tribune* warned about those "who try to excuse this and other actions as . . . part of the crime."[8] In a similar vein, the New York *Post* warned readers that "violence is the order of the day. The North is to be pushed to the wall by it and this plot will succeed if the people of the free states are as apathetic as the slave holders are insolent."[9] A week later, the *Post* offered a bit of sarcasm about how Brooks was being greeted as a hero in the South. It printed a fictitious letter that one "Bill Sikes"—named after the villain from Charles Dickens's *Oliver Twist*—had supposedly written from New York's Sing Sing prison. If Brooks, a common criminal, was to be treated as a hero, said Sikes, then he, too, should be so honored.[10]

The Republican Albany *Evening Journal,* edited by the politically powerful Thurlow Weed, began its report of the incident by declaring that South Carolina had its barbarians, as did ancient Israel. The caning of Charles Sumner meant that the "extreme discipline of the Plantation has been introduced into the Senate."[11] The *Journal* described Senator Butler of South Carolina as "insolent, dictatorial and contemptuous with the voice and temper of an overseer." The incident proved that the South would use violence to preserve and to extend slavery.[12] The Philadelphia *Ledger and Transcript* characterized Brooks's use of force as an assault on all "rights and liberties" and denounced his tactics as those of a "low ruffian."[13]

Writing from Sumner's hometown, the Boston *Evening Transcript*'s reaction was typical of those presented in northern newspapers supporting the Republican Party. The *Transcript* began a long editorial by referring to the event as a "cowardly and brutal assault" and later in the piece labeled it "an attempted murder." Sumner was described as a "statesman and a patriot" and as a "high toned gentleman." The newspaper acknowledged that he had verbally attacked his opponents but explained that "they had scandalously assaulted him in the Senate for the last two years." Readers were assured that Sumner had "already proved himself the superior in knowledge, in eloquence, and in genius" of men such as Butler and Douglas.[14]

In short, in the arena of political debate—in the war of words, ideas, and logic—those opponents were no match for Sumner, and so it was no wonder, given the southern character, that friends of Butler and Douglas would resort to violence just as they had been doing in Kansas. Brooks's name was not used in the story. (Perhaps anonymity for the assailant suggested that any and all southerners could be expected to behave in a such a fashion.) When Brooks was discussed, he was portrayed as part of a conspiratorial group that had started the bloodshed in Kansas and now carried that mode of attack into the halls of Congress. The *Transcript* described such men as "barbarians engaged in crimes not merely against liberty but against civilization."[15] The clear implication was that Sumner was the defender of both liberty and civilization, and for that reason the barbarian southerners saw him as a threat, "an unsafe man for them," so they had to silence him. Having so indicted southerners, the *Transcript* confidently announced that "we trust we shall hear no more of Southern chivalry." So much for southern "respectability."[16]

The accusations put before the *Transcript*'s readers, as well as readers of many other northern newspapers, conjured up images of the virtues displayed by some Americans and the vices displayed by others. The press in both regions used labels such as "barbarians" and "civilized people" but with a reversal of roles, depending on the region. Slavery, pro or con, provided the inflammatory source, but the true question, the key point, was what slavery and antislavery conveyed to the public about the character of the people of each region. The northern press's focus on Brooks's assault on Sumner was that it revealed the true and barbaric nature of the southern character. If, as the *National Intelligencer* had written, this was a nothing more than a dispute rooted in a personal matter, why had it not been settled in a way that civilized men settle disputes?

Although dueling was illegal in most states and in the District of Columbia, duels still were being fought and might have been expected in this case. Because Brooks was Butler's nephew, and because Butler, even if he had been there to defend his own honor, was too old and sickly to have done so, under long-held gentlemen's codes it became Brooks's duty to act. His friends reminded him of that duty on the first day of Sumner's two-day oration.[17] Brooks understood what his duty was but was uncertain of either the appropriate punishment or how and where best to inflict it. Were Sumner to apologize, that would end the matter. But Brooks knew Sumner would not do that. Brooks also considered challenging Sumner to a duel, with little risk to Brooks because Sumner would never have engaged in such uncivilized behavior. Brooks was not without experience in dueling, which was considered well within the bounds of civilized behavior in South Carolina. He already had fought a duel and, in fact, made two challenges in the week following the caning incident. He challenged two Massachusetts legislators, Sen. Henry Wilson and Rep. Anson Burlingame. Wilson refused to accept the challenge, and although Burlingame accepted the demand for satisfaction the duel was never fought. Burlingame insisted that they meet in a northern locale, but Brooks refused to travel, saying that he feared assassination en route.[18]

While Brooks apparently considered Wilson and Burlingame to be gentlemen, the South Carolina Congressman wrote to his brother that he chose not to challenge Sumner because the Massachusetts senator was not a gentleman and thus was not his social equal. Brooks chose instead to thrash Sumner with a stick.[19] He made clear to his brother that his intent was to whip Sumner but not kill him. Brooks chose to punish Sumner in a way consistent with the manner in which a southern planter and a gentleman would treat someone beneath him in rank and station. The caning was meant to take place in the street, a place befitting dealing with a scoundrel, but Brooks could not find Sumner outside the Capitol on either May 21 or May 22, when he sought to confront the senator. Frustrated and determined to act promptly, Brooks entered the Senate chamber and waited for the session to end. When it did, Sumner remained at his desk while a few other senators in the chamber engaged in conversation. Although their presence did not trouble Brooks, the presence of ladies in the gallery did because a gentleman would never thrash someone in front of ladies.[20] It was an hour before the gallery cleared and Brooks could proceed.

These details of Brooks's motives and behavior received little or no notice in the northern press, but they were carried in detail in southern newspapers. At issue was whether Brooks had behaved like a gentleman. Although historians have documented well the southern preoccupation with honor, northerners, too, worried about the defense of honor.[21] The importance of honor, and the need to defend honor and satisfy real or perceived insults to honor, was, as it had been from the early days of the Republic, a national trait evidenced by those who considered themselves to be gentlemen. Honor was both a matter of pride and of practical importance in the Republic, because it served as a form of self-regulation of behavior. Without honor, liberty would either lead to anarchy or be infringed for the sake of order. Honor, liberty, and the Republic were all connected, one to the other. Belief that a republican form of government could work rested on the character of the people of that republic. Concern over flaws, current or potential, in the public character had been evident in both the South and the North since the Republic's founding.

As newspapers described it, the Brooks-Sumner incident was first and foremost a comment on and a warning about the character of a people. If virtue gave way to vice, if civilization gave way to barbarism, and if Americans became creatures controlled by their passions, the Republic was lost. As was clear in the newspapers, civic virtue and honor were important topics of discussion and concern for Americans in 1856. The civilized society in which a republic could thrive was an orderly system, whereas a barbaric society, the result of the triumph of passion over reason, would be anarchical. Over and over it was expected, and called for, that reason, and thus civilization, would prevail over passion and its accompanying savagery.

In an American society built on the premise and promise of liberty for its people, there was ongoing tension that grew over time. Slaveholders as well as many non-slaveholders, both north and south, viewed slaves as creatures less than human and so not entitled to liberty. Themes of liberty versus order were woven through the columns of newspapers throughout the nation. Bundles of disquieting issues, not all directly apparent in the newspapers day by day, added tension to society. These included the growing commercialization of society, the uncertainties of social status and economic well-being, and, to many, a threatening growth in the number of immigrants, the increasing diversity of religious faiths, and even the invention of new faiths such as Mormonism.

Overall, it was clear that there was an increasing visibility of groups of people who sought, or who simply by their presence would produce, radical changes in society. Taken together, all these tensions created an environment in which demands for the extension of liberty had to be weighed against fear of social anarchy.[22] Obedience to laws and respect for property as well as honorable behavior were more important than ever. Americans of both regions were troubled by questions of when order became oppression and when liberty became license. When laws were violated, could such violations be justified in terms of the dictates of some higher law? What then would be the consequences of such behavior?

Even acknowledging the importance of societal stresses over the massive influx of immigration, a growing number of Roman Catholics and the debate over temperance heightened tensions and produced changes in political allegiances for some Americans, north and south. Nevertheless, based on what was in the newspapers, slavery—more than anything else—was what produced the lacerating distrust, name-calling, and demonizing hatred that together constituted the ingredients necessary to produce a climate in which civil war seemed a valid option.

The Boston *Evening Transcript*'s account of the slavery-related Brooks-Sumner incident made clear that southerners were ruffians. Southerners had shown their lawless character in Kansas, and now they were displaying their penchant for violence against a duly elected representative of Massachusetts. Implicit in the newspaper's coverage was the question of what lawlessness would occur next. Although the violence in Kansas could be attributed to some of society's lesser sorts—common criminals—the South Carolina "ruffian" was himself a duly elected public official. The *Transcript* warned that southern politicians who were making the nation's laws, and were indeed the controlling force in the national government, were the "border brethren" of the Missouri ruffians, a reference to proslavery men who crossed from that slave state into the Kansas Territory. What would become of political institutions and a government of laws in the hands of such men? The newspaper concluded that without civilized men in control of government, neither liberty nor order were safe.[23]

As described in northern newspapers, the attack on Sumner in the halls of Congress showed arrogance of power along with southerners' distrust for government, even when they controlled it. The New York *Enquirer* headlined a piece on the incident as "The Bullying of the Slave Owner," and the New York *Times* labeled Sumner's speech as one of the ablest ever made and the speaker an "'honorable member who at no time went beyond the limits of parliamentary propriety.'"[24] The *Times* also described Brooks's attack as a "brutal outrage." As newspapers in general shaped the argument, although slavery prompted the conflict between Brooks and Sumner, it was the very character of the American people and the nature of their society that were the important issues for northerners as well as southerners.

As the Republican press told readers, the southern barbarians' threat to the Republic, which was evident in the flawed characters of such men, was clear in Brooks's behavior. To demonstrate that this was no isolated incident, those northern newspapers that were sympathetic to Sumner naturally picked up on the reference in his speech to the history of the people of Butler's home state. The press joined Sumner in portraying South Carolina as the land of the Tories in the 1770s, nullificationists in the 1830s, and the hotbed of secessionists in the 1850s. South Carolinians were described as "ultras" or, to use a term even more inflammatory to northern newspaper readers, "insurrectionists." South Carolina men such as Brooks were traitors who came from a long line of traitors. Sumner's accusations that South Carolinians had failed to support the Republic since the time of the Revolution was a stinging indictment. South Carolinians were so portrayed by the editors who shared his views.

In editorializing on the incident, Horace Greeley's Republican New York *Tribune* declared that there was a need to save the country from the "infidelity to the Revolutionary tradition."[25] Sumner claimed that only a handful of South Carolinians had fought to make the Republic, as opposed to many thousands of Massachusetts men, and thus there was clear evidence that when Senator Butler spoke it was with the voice of someone who had no respect for the Revolutionary heritage.

The Republican press portrayed Brooks the same way. It ignored the fact that he, like all other South Carolina politicians of the time, supported secession as a concept. In fact, Brooks was one of a group of that state's representatives in the House who saw secession only as a last resort, much preferring compromise and with it continued loyalty to the Union.[26] Even if his words denied it, to most northern newspapers his caning of Sumner made him a "fire-eater," a label used both by some northern and southern newspapers for those southerners intent on protecting and promoting their region's interest even if it meant sacrificing the Republic.

Shortly after the caning, the New York *Tribune* carried excerpts from a sermon by the famous Presbyterian minister Henry Ward Beecher, delivered from the pulpit of his Brooklyn, New York, church. The *Tribune,* with its daily and weekly publications adding up to the nation's largest circulation, quoted Beecher's description of Sumner as "a martyr for the cause of human liberty." Beecher, brother of the even more famous Harriet Beecher Stowe, author of *Uncle Tom's Cabin,* went on to plead that "we must put love of freedom above love of money."[27] Among other things, Beecher was jabbing at New York merchants whose trade with the South was a vital factor in their economic success and who were ready to offer any concession to keep southern customers happy. The Republican press used direct attacks on the Republic by those whose history was said to be replete with evidence of opposition to it to alert readers to the dangers of a loss of patriotic fervor. Now it was time for defenders of the Revolutionary heritage to show their patriotism, demonstrate their "manliness," and stand up for the Republic against "Bully Brooks" and the "bullying Slaveocracy."[28]

Readers of the majority of northern newspapers were presented with a list of southern character flaws that Brooks's act proved. The press described southerners as barbarians rather than civilized, as selfish rather than selfless, and as lawless rather than respectful of law. The southern press drew diametrically different conclusions from the incident. It considered the Brooks attack on Sumner as a case of righting the wrongs done to Brooks's kinsmen and to all southerners. To that element of the northern press sympathetic to the South and to the southern press, the incident demonstrated all the evils and provoked all the concerns it did for northerners, but with roles reversed.

In the wake of the Brooks-Sumner incident, the usually Democratic and pro-southern New York *Herald* scolded Brooks for his behavior and cautioned that such actions cast the South in a bad light in the North. The *Herald* warned that unless extremists such as Brooks and Sumner were checked the country was headed toward "mob law and destruction of the Union."[29] Editor James Gordon Bennett saw the slavery issue, once the weapon only of fanatics, as now being used for personal gain by "unscrupulous politicians from both sections." In an age in which newspaper editors were unrestrained in their rhetoric, none could outdo Bennett. He brutally characterized the new political forces at work, represented on one side by Brooks and on the other by Sumner, as "nigger drivers in the South and nigger lovers in the North." In an editorial two days after the incident, the *Herald* declared that the Democratic Party was now controlled by the former and the Whigs by the latter. A third party, Bennett insisted, was needed, a new party that would represent what he termed the "conservative mass" of people of both sections who wanted no part of such extremism. Moreover, the people must reject those politicians who claimed popular support in their respective regions "based on their stance on the nigger question."[30]

Although most newspapers took a clear stand about the right or wrong of what had happened, the *Herald* was one of a number of northern Democratic publications that chastised Sumner for his provocative language and found reasons to excuse Brooks for acting as he did. The Democratic Cincinnati *Enquirer* denounced Sumner's attack on South Carolinians, especially his claim that they were Tories. The *Enquirer* was also critical of Brooks for the way he punished Sumner but made it clear that the Massachusetts senator deserved punishment. The Cincinnati newspaper warned that Sumner could provoke war just as surely as could the abolitionists in Kansas.[31] Another Democratic newspaper in a border area, the *Democrat* of St. Louis, also warned of the impact of the Brooks-Sumner incident on the climate of public opinion: "It is but another ingredient in the boiling cauldron—another symptom of the sectional animosity which burns beneath the surface of society." The editor concluded by asserting, "The blood of Northern men is up and the blood of Southern men is never down." Southern men were "ruled by passion," and passion was the enemy of civilization and hence the Republic.[32] In Abraham Lincoln's hometown, Springfield, Illinois, the *Illinois State Register* described Sumner's behavior in the harshest possible terms, calling him "a base lying blackguard, a bully without courage, a peace man [Sumner was a pacifist] and a blusterer, a provoker of fights and a non-resistant upshot." Moreover, the Massachusetts senator, the tirade continued, was "a heterogenous conglomeration of everything knavish, mean and cowardly."[33]

Although the Louisville *Journal* denounced Brooks's behavior, attributing it to the nature of South Carolinians and noting the long history of violence there, the Kentucky newspaper nevertheless made clear that "we have no sympathy for Sumner." The newspaper insisted, "He has deported himself as a pestilent enemy of the peace and harmony of the country."[34] Writing from Georgia, the Milledgeville *Federal Union* conceded that the "whipping" Brooks gave Sumner would serve to embarrass the South, especially because it was administered in the Senate chamber, but nevertheless applauded the act. By way of justification, the *Union* castigated Sumner for "that compound of vulgarity, abuse and falsehood called a speech, in which he knew he violated the laws of decency." The *Union*'s editor described the speech as "one of the most malignant and indecent tirades ever uttered in the Senate Chamber." The editorial concluded with the assertion that the speech was far more threatening to the Republic than was the whipping or he who delivered it. Finally, in response to Sumner's attack on South Carolinians' loyalty to the Republic, the *Union* claimed that men from Massachusetts had no right to complain, "for she has a long time been without the pale of the Constitution and the laws of the Union by virtue of an act of her own legislature."[35] This was a reference to the Commonwealth's refusal to enforce the Fugitive Slave Act that was part of the Compromise of 1850.

Although the Louisville and Milledgeville newspapers, each in its own way, offered some slight condemnation of Brooks, for most of the press south of the Mason and Dixon line he was a hero and Sumner a villain, with no equivocation expressed on the matter. Sumner's crimes and Brooks's virtue reflected in almost every respect the same concerns as those expressed in the northern press but reversed them. In a brief note, one South Carolina newspaper referred to the incident as "a genteel caning" and cried, "Well done Col. Brooks."[36] In a bit more statesmanlike approach, another South Carolina newspaper, after denouncing Sumner's character, regretted that "it has become necessary for the defenders of the South to throw aside argument and sound reason, the weapons of honorable high-minded combat, and to resort in their stead to the argument of cow-hide in avenging insult and protecting his own and the honor of those whom they represent." Brooks, it insisted, had acted "gallantly."[37]

On May 28, 1856, the Charleston *Courier* took the offensive by reporting that at a recent meeting of the women of that city it had been agreed to provide Brooks with "hickory sticks with which to chastise Abolitionists and Red Republicans." The Charleston editor went on to note that in Columbia, South Carolina, "the slaves . . . have raised money for him . . . for his preservation and the protection of their rights and enjoyments as the happiest laborers on the face of the globe." For the more openly secessionist Charleston *Mercury,* the incident should have made it clear to all, north and south, that rhetoric had given way to action—and it was about time. Edmund Ruffin, the editor, insisted that "the South certainly has become generally convinced that it is by hard blows, and not by loud blustering and insulting denunciation, that the sectional ground is to be settled."[38] That, he noted proudly, had been the *Mercury*'s position for twenty years.

The Richmond, Virginia, *Enquirer* was widely read and also often quoted in the northern press. On June 3, 1856, nearly two weeks after the celebrated caning, the *Enquirer* set forth what amounted to a counterattack. It published its interpretation of the incident and offered an impassioned rejoinder to those northern papers that had seen the incident as a flagrant violation of freedom of speech. The *Enquirer* labeled Sumner a typical abolitionist and declared that his kind were the real threat to liberty—to freedom of speech, the press, and religion. The *Enquirer* began its attack by asserting that "Liberty is only desirable so long as it is enjoyed without abuse. It is the highest evidence of the morality, piety, intelligence and general well-being of peoples and individuals, that they require but little legal restraint." Turning to the northern arguments that Brooks's actions were evidence of southern barbarism and that such behavior would bring an end to the Republic in which liberty was possible only so long as public virtue existed, the *Enquirer* characterized northern abolitionists as the barbaric force endangering liberty. Although liberty was good in the hands of virtuous people, it could be "an unmitigated evil to the vicious, who use their privileges to injure themselves, and to annoy and disturb society." The editor also argued that while abolitionists accused slaveholders of despotism, it actually was the abolitionists who were the despots. "The Northern Abolitionists do not let a day pass without showing the world that they are as little fitted to be trusted with liberty as thieves with keys or children with firearms."

The *Enquirer,* having told readers that abolitionists were the worst abusers and enemies of liberty, then described them as men, women, and blacks who were the worst sort of social radicals and behaved in "disgusting" fashion and championed wildly anarchic causes. "A community of Abolitionists could only be governed by a penitentiary system. They are as unfit for liberty as maniacs, criminals, or wild beasts." While abolitionists and their northern sympathizers might cry that Sumner's right to free speech was violated, "they [would] soon destroy all liberty of speech, if they employ it only to teach heresy, infidelity, licentiousness, and stir up deeds of violence."[39] The editor lumped abolitionists with advocates of women's rights, free love, Mormonism, the Oneida community, and Catholicism. For the *Enquirer* and presumably its readers, that was a combination of evils of the worst kind, the greatest threat to a virtuous people who were the foundation of a successful republic. The piece concluded with some assurances that these "wretches are mostly more noisy than numerous." The *Enquirer* insisted that the Republic was safe from "the assaults of crazy Lilliputians" and that, as demonstrated by election victories of northern

Democrats, abolitionists would "be soon driven from their places, and lashed into obscurity by an indignant people, whose confidence they have betrayed and abused."[40]

The *Enquirer*'s Richmond competitor, the *Whig,* commented in a May 31 editorial on the reports coming from Washington of Sumner's poor condition following the attack. Those reports, the *Whig* declared, were "all very strange and funny, and lead us to believe that the Abolition wretch, with his Abolition physicians as accomplices in the trick, is playing *possum.*" The *Whig* accepted accounts indicating that Sumner had been injured but could not imagine him needing even a week to recover. It also reiterated the claim that his prolonged absence from Senate was a ruse "to keep alive and diffuse and strengthen the sympathy awakened for him among his confederates at the North, Nigger-worshiping fanatics of the male gender, and weak-minded women and silly children who are horribly affected at the thought of blood oozing from a pin-scratch." The editor concluded by accusing Sumner of acting the role of wily politician and at the same time demonstrating cowardice by remaining away from his desk.

Republican newspapers, in the months and years that followed the incident, described Sumner as a tough, manly, and heroic victim of a cowardly attacker. In the northern Democratic and southern press, however, he was pictured as the cowardly receiver of a much-deserved thrashing whose three-year absence from the Senate was proof of cowardice and/or evidence of sinister behavior.

The rhetoric of newspapers, north and south, Whig, Republican, and Democratic, evoked images of civilized or barbaric men, of courage and cowardice, of manliness or timidity, of defense of honor or promotion of reckless violence, and of the championing of republican liberty or despotic destruction of that liberty. The incident had set the dispute over slavery in the territories in a different context. This was not just a quarrel between greedy settlers in a new land or a contest between rival politicians. More serious than that, it was about the American character and the fate of the Republic, and it was played out for the American people in the newspapers that were the primary source of information for most readers. The words used by Sumner and other politicians and their antagonists and the words in newspapers perhaps symbolized a change in communication patterns. Historian Andrew W. Robertson has contended that the content and style of rhetoric of both politicians and newspapers changed with the democratization of American politics in striving to reach mass audiences. Robertson concluded that Sumner was speaking not so much to fellow senators as to the nation's newspapers—its mass media.

3   The *Dred Scott* Decision and a Society of Laws

In the summer months of 1856, with the Brooks-Sumner incident no longer hot news, the press turned its attention back to Kansas. While pro- and antislavery supporters continued to pour verbal abuse on one another, particularly through the newspapers, a new round of violence broke out. The violence was centered along the Wakarusa River near the town of Lawrence. There, the preceding spring, a proslavery force had attacked the predominantly antislavery community, burning, looting, and killing some of its residents. The new confrontation saw some fifteen hundred supporters of slavery gather in the area. Before a major conflict could occur, the territorial governor managed to calm the situation. But anyone who read a newspaper was aware of "Bleeding Kansas." It was in that charged atmosphere that the justices of the Supreme Court of the United States were deliberating a long-standing dispute that, although not set in Kansas, would have important implications for tensions there and in any place in the country where the question of the right of one person to hold another in bondage might be raised. By late winter of 1857 the Court rendered a decision in the case of *Dred Scott v. Sanford*.

On March 4, 1857, Chief Justice of the Supreme Court Roger Taney administered the presidential oath of office to James Buchanan, a Democrat from Pennsylvania. Two days later, the eighty-one-year-old chief justice, speaking in a voice so weak it was barely audible, announced the decision of the Court's majority in a case that had been working its way through local, state, and federal courts for a decade and had been heard for a second time by the highest court.[1] The case involved a suit brought by a slave named Dred Scott against his owner. Scott's lawyers claimed that because his master at one time had taken him to live in Illinois, a free state, he was entitled to freedom.

Although a majority of the justices joined Taney in rejecting Scott's claim, two dissented: Benjamin Curtis of Massachusetts, the first to write his opinion, and John McLean of New York, who put forth his dissenting view a few days after Curtis. Chief Justice Taney's formal written opinion for the majority did not appear for several months. The Court's decision, however, was known nationwide in early March because of the presence of an Associated Press reporter who took down what the chief justice said in delivering the majority opinion. The actual outcome thus was reported in newspapers across the country.

The Court majority found that because he was a slave, Dred Scott was property and not a person. Therefore, Scott had no standing to sue for his freedom. Taney and his colleagues might have stopped there, but they chose to deal with slavery in the Territories, an issue being debated at the time. Did Congress now or at any time in the past have the power to restrict slaveholders from taking their property (i.e., their slaves) to any territory of the United States? The Northwest Ordinance of 1789 and the Missouri Compromise of 1820 had both restricted that right, and the recently passed Kansas-Nebraska Act enabled a majority of voters in any territory to restrict the right of slave owners to transport their slaves to their territory.

In its decision, the Court majority declared those federal legislative acts to be unconstitutional and by inference questioned the constitutionality of state laws prohibiting slavery. The majority sought by its decision to put to rest a profoundly divisive issue that had troubled the nation for the thirty-seven years since the Missouri Compromise, an issue that threatened the future of the Republic. Taney and his colleagues voting in the majority, five from the South and two from the North, acted to assure slaveholders that whatever happened politically, whoever should control the federal government, the law protected the institution of slavery.

Taney and the other justices who agreed with him hoped that with southern fears regarding slavery quieted there would be no reason for the South to leave the Union nor any further reason why the confrontation between northerners and southerners would continue.[2] As these jurists saw it, slavery would cease to be an issue, and abolitionists would be reduced to an ineffectual group of extremists whose objectives could be attained only through unlawful means. Political parties, in particular the Democratic Party, Taney's party, could successfully push the slavery question off the table, as was done in the days of Andrew Jackson, and free itself from the demands of dissident factions. But the justices badly misread the temper of the times.

While the Court's decision pleased most southern newspaper editors who recognized that the Court finally had acknowledged what proslavery advocates had always insisted, that slaves were property and that property rights were sacred, many a southern editor warned readers that northern "fanatics" would reject the decision and so the authority of the Court to interpret the Constitution. Although moderate southern newspapers and most northern Democratic ones urged readers to accept the Court's ruling and see the *Dred Scott* decision as the basis on which to end debate over issues related to slavery, other northern editors described the decision as further proof that the southern minority was engaged in a conspiracy to control the country.

In the case of the Brooks-Sumner incident, some northern newspapers had claimed that northerners were law-abiding and that southerners acted outside the law. In the case of the *Dred Scott* decision, the roles were reversed. It would be southern papers that declared their readers to be obedient to the law of the land and demanded respect for the Constitution as the Supreme Court interpreted it. As those southern, and some northern, newspapers saw it, by rejecting a Supreme Court decision those northerners threatened to ignore the law of the land and were endangering the well-being of the Republic.

While northern Democratic newspapers shared the hope of the Court majority that the decision would end the divisive debates over slavery, the Republican press lashed out at the decision and the men who made it as either lackeys to or active allies of the slave-power conspirators. Among the attackers was Thurlow Weed and his Albany, New York, *Evening Journal*.

For three decades Weed had used whatever newspaper he edited to declare that there was irrefutable evidence of some conspiracy to destroy the Republic. Then, having made the allegation, Weed's newspaper would crusade against the supposed conspirators and support those political figures who sided with him in the battle. In 1826, as an editor in western New York, Weed had sensationalized the arrest and kidnaping of William Morgan, who had threatened to publish the secret rituals of the Masonic fraternity. Weed used the incident to encourage formation of the Anti-Masonic Party.[3] Later, the New Yorker played an important role in the formation of the Whig Party, decrying what he claimed was the Democratic conspiracy to put a crown on Andrew Jackson. Now, with *Dred Scott,* Weed had found a new conspiracy to attack. Replying to the report of Taney's decision in the case, the *Evening Journal,* after summarizing the decision in one short paragraph, announced on March 9, 1857, that "it is no novelty to find the Supreme Court following the lead of the Slavery Extension party, [the Democrats] to which most of its members belong. Five of the judges are slave holders and two of the other four owe their appointments to their facile ingenuity in making State laws bend to Federal demands on behalf of the Southern institution."[4]

The *Journal*'s editorial began with the declaration that "the three hundred and forty-seven thousand five hundred and twenty-five Slave holders in the Republic, accomplished day before yesterday a great success—as shallow men estimate success. They converted the Supreme Court of Law and Equity of the United States of America into a propagandist of human slavery. Fatal day for a judiciary made reputable throughout the world, and reliable to all in this nation, by the learning and the virtues of Jay, Rutledge, Ellsworth, Marshall and Story!"[5] The point was clear. The members of this minority—all 347,525 of them—had used the Supreme Court to impose their will on thirty million Americans. The current justices, pallid shadows of those who had served so well before them, had protected the interests of that minority at the expense of the interest of the majority.

"The conspiracy is nearly completed," Weed continued. "The legislation of the Republic is in the hands of this handful of Slave holders." With Buchanan just inaugurated as president, the Senate in Democratic Party hands, and now this Court decision, slaveholders were now in control of all branches of government. After reviewing the *Dred Scott* decision, Weed asserted that readers could next expect the Court to rule that "slaves can lawfully be held in Free States, and slavery be fully maintained here in New York through the sanctions of 'property' contained in the Constitution." Although the *Dred Scott* decision did not specify that slaves could be held in a state that had declared slavery to be illegal, the implication was clear to northern Republicans that slavery was unleashed and as a result New York, Massachusetts, or any other northern state could become a battleground between free and slave labor.

Having declared a crisis to be at hand and a conspiracy to be on the brink of success, Weed issued a challenge to readers and a warning to the South:

> Beneath Courts and Congresses and Presidents is the great PEOPLE. They love liberty—they love justice—they love humanity. Till they affirm the decisions of Law embattling man's divine nature, and till they approve of legislation which defies God, and till they order Executives to execute inequity, this conspiracy of the Oligarchy is wholly incomplete. That consent will forever and ever be wanting. But one thing will not be wanting—the resolute purpose of the humane, the just and the free men of the free States, to meet the close issue forced upon them through the decision of the case of Dred, squarely and fairly, and never to abate their efforts to recover the entire administration away from Slavery and back again to Freedom.[6]

The *Evening Journal* concluded its challenge by declaring, "All who love Republican institutions and who hate Aristocracy, compact yourselves together for the struggle which threatens your liberty and will test your manhood."

Like Weed's long-time New York political friend and ally William Seward, who declared that the country faced an irrepressible conflict, the editor had declared political war. Weed insisted that people had to vote the Republicans into power to gain control of the executive, legislative, and, by new appointments of justices, judicial branches of government. Moreover, they had to use that power to defeat the conspiratorial efforts of the slave-power aristocracy.

Republican editor Horace Greeley of the New York *Daily Tribune,* writing on March 10, 1857, took up the subject of Dred Scott. After reporting the decision as gleaned from the pages of the Washington, D.C., *National Intelligencer,* which had first carried Taney's remarks, Greeley declared the chief justice's opinion to be "but a mere collation of false statements and shallow sophistries, got together to sustain a foregone conclusion—knowing that he was engaged in a pitiful attempt to impose upon the public." Heating up his attack on the opinion and on Taney, Greeley charged that "downright and bare-faced falsehood is its main staple. Any slave-driving editor or Virginia bar-room politician could have taken the Chief Justice's place on the bench, and with the exception of a little bolder speaking up, nobody would have perceived the difference."

Having denounced the opinion, and he who rendered it, the *Tribune*'s editor then addressed the key points of the decision. As for the claim that the Constitution barred blacks from ever being citizens, Greeley dismissed the Court's argument that they were so treated as inference based on no facts. This was, he insisted, no legal opinion; it was more like a political stump speech. In the decision Taney had argued that, to the Founding Fathers, it was axiomatic that blacks were inferior beings who could only be property and never be citizens. Greeley insisted that the Founders had no such understanding. Whatever the practice of the time, Thomas Jefferson had written in the Declaration of Independence about self-evident truths, and one of those truths was that all men were created equal. At the time of independence there were free black people in America who exercised full rights as citizens. Whatever the Founders' view regarding whether blacks could be citizens, the *Tribune* insisted that the Constitution could not and was not intended to restrict states from passing laws governing slavery. With this use of a states' rights argument, Greeley ended his attack on the decision by applauding the dissenting views of Justices Benjamin Curtis and John McLean.

In a March 16, 1857, editorial, the *Tribune* dismissed the Court and the majority decision as "extra-judicial." The manhood of readers was challenged by noting the threat to northerners implicit in the decision: "If we do not all quietly submit to the recent gratuitous attempt on the part of five slaveholding Judges to remodel the Constitution of the United States so as to make it suit their individual wishes or those of the section to which they belong we are threatened with being hung, drawn or quartered and guilty of high treason." The *Tribune* had declared the decision invalid and decried in the harshest terms those who made it.

In Washington, D.C., the Republican *National Era* labeled the Court a "bulwark of Slavery."[7] After summarizing the decision, the *Era* then asked, "What is to be done? It is useless to rail and denounce; the crisis calls for action." Further, "The Slave holding Oligarchy have the Administration, the majority in the Senate and in the House and the Supreme Court." As Weed and Greeley had done, the *Era*'s editor called on the people to overthrow the "Oligarchy" through the ballot box. If they did not, the newspaper warned, "They will have made up . . . their minds to be the political slaves of the slave holders, and to see this American Union dedicated to the spread and support of Slave holding Institutions, as its great mission."

Farther West, Republican newspapers' views of the Court decision mirrored those of their northeastern colleagues. In Pittsburgh, the editor of the Republican *Gazette* took the Court's decision as a challenge and a call to action. "It will awaken the friends of freedom to renewed efforts."[8] The Chicago *Tribune* warned readers that the Court decision "sweeps away all the legislation of the Fathers against the extension of Slavery." The editor declared that the Court had given southern extremists their way and that southern calls for equality for their region masked "efforts at despotism." Once again conspiracy theory was evident as the *Tribune* warned that the Court was "part of a grand conspiracy against freedom." Like other Republican newspapers, the *Tribune* used the term *oligarchy* to describe the southern minority; like its namesake in New York it also concluded by describing the decision as an important step toward "making slavery the law of the Republic."[9] As for the question of what to do about the situation, the editor urged all newspapers to publish Taney's decision so the public would become aware of the southern threat and vote in the Republicans to protect them from it.

In Milwaukee, Wisconsin, Sherman Booth, an avowed antislavery advocate, had his say. Booth, who later was jailed for aiding a fugitive slave, was editor of the Milwaukee *Free Democrat.* He responded predictably to the *Dred Scott* decision with dire forecasts of what now lay ahead. Booth began his March 7, 1857, editorial on the case by describing the decision as "the most important political document that has been published in this country since the foundation of the government." He labeled the Court decision a "counter-revolution" and then stated that the decision seemed to set aside state laws barring slavery and so had "established slavery in every part of the Union." By so doing, Booth insisted, "It has subverted the public liberties of the nation. It has made the entire Union the home of the slave." The *Free Democrat* called on its readers to abolish the Court because the Court had abolished the Constitution. Booth concluded with fiery words: "Freedom has been declared unconstitutional."

In the border state of Missouri, the editor of the *Missouri Democrat,* a Republican publication in St. Louis, although giving the decision less space than the other Republican newspapers, seemed no less angry about what the Court had done. The *Democrat* labeled the decision a revocation of policies established by the Founding Fathers and, like the other Republican newspapers, declared slavery now to be national. That version of the conspiracy theory was set forth in the words "the supreme power which has not only the executive and all the legislative, but even the judicial department of government under its feet."[10]

Taney and his colleagues had some support in the North and, of course, throughout the South. Newspapers that supported the decision quickly came to the defense of the Court and castigated all who questioned the decision and challenged the legitimacy of the Court. That segment of the press argued that if the nation's ultimate arbiter of the law and interpreter of the Constitution was discredited, what hope would there be of maintaining order, avoiding anarchy, and saving the Republic? As the editor of the Augusta, Georgia, *Constitutionalist* put it, "'Southern opinion upon the subject of southern slavery . . . is now the supreme law of the land . . . and opposition to southern opinion upon this subject is now opposition to the Constitution and morally treason against the government.'"[11] Would that element of the northern press and the northern public that supported the Republican Party accept this state of things? Would the Republican press that denounced the decision, and those who made it, succeed in persuading their reading public that nothing less than northern manhood in service to the Republic had been challenged and that both that manhood and the future of the Republic were at stake? Not if the pro-Democratic northern press could prevent it.

The New York *Herald* leaped to the defense of the *Dred Scott* decision and to the attack against the position of its rival, the New York *Daily Tribune.*[12] James Gordon Bennett, who since taking over the *Herald* in the 1830s had been sympathetic to southern interests, was determined to prevent the issue of slavery from interfering with what he deemed the progress of the American republic. As Bennett continued to put the matter, neither the "nigger drivers nor the nigger worshipers" could be allowed to control public opinion and hence control the course of events.[13] The publisher labeled those people as fanatics and as a minority in their respective regions of the country. As he saw it, "practical men" looked at the impending crisis as a pragmatic matter rather than a dispute over vague and divisive principles. He believed firmly that northerners "should concede anything to slavery in order to conciliate the South and save the Union."[14] Bennett had no doubt that ideologies—of whatever sort—would be the Republic's undoing.

Bennett's first reading of the account of the Taney opinion in the *Dred Scott* case as it came into the *Herald*'s office over the telegraph delighted him. On March 6, 1857, the same day that Taney delivered his report on the majority decision, the *Herald* editorialized on the case. It applauded Taney and the Court majority and noted hopefully, "They cover all the disturbing party and sectional issues upon the slavery controversy, and strike at the root of the mischief in every case." Bennett asserted that the decision killed antislavery and any efforts in Congress to act against slaveholders. The Court had now resolved that issue. President James Buchanan could get on with the business of governing the country, and the country could get on with its business of growing in wealth and power without the unwanted interference of the slavery debate.

But as early as March 12, 1857, undoubtedly inspired by critical editorials in the New York *Tribune,* the *Herald* returned to defending the decision and to denouncing those who denounced it. In that March 12 edition, the *Herald* announced that "the Court has spoken and their position must be accepted." It reiterated its often-stated belief, now agreed to by the Supreme Court, that slaves were not and could not be citizens and that notions of equality of the races would doom America. It also conceded, however, that "the issues are not settled for all time but at least for now." Bennett warned that if Republicans came to power in 1860 the slavery issue would resurface.

By March 14, the *Herald* expressed fear that rather than the Court having settled the matter, even temporarily, it may have produced even greater sectional strife. The *Herald* attributed the cause of the strife to those in the North who would not accept the Court's decision. The next day, March 15, taking particular note of the *Tribune*'s attacks on the decision and the Court that rendered it, Bennett declared the *Tribune*'s stance on the *Dred Scott* decision to be "brimful of the elements of sedition, treason, and insurrection." He accused Horace Greeley and all Republicans of rejecting the law of the land, noting that it was the law whether they liked it or not. The *Herald* argued that the response to the decision proved that Republicans were really abolitionists.

Democratic newspapers in other free states joined Bennett in praising Taney and his colleagues who constituted the majority. In its March 10 issue, the Cincinnati *Enquirer* told readers that, at the time of the Missouri Compromise, "our fathers trusted too much to time, patriotism and nationalism and unduly under-estimated the power and influence of fanaticism and sectionalism." The *Dred Scott* decision would save the country from that "fanaticism and sectionalism," and that it served as "the olive branch they've needed." But for many southern and some northern papers this was no peace offering. As they saw it, the *Dred Scott* decision was a definitive—indeed, decisive—triumph over northern abolitionists and their growing numbers of fellow travelers.

The Springfield, Illinois, *State Register* claimed on March 12 that the decision was a total victory over the Black Republicans (a term used often by opponents of the Republican Party to link it to abolitionists and all who opposed slavery), who, the editor insisted, cared less for the sanctity of the Constitution than for the restoration of the Missouri Compromise. As the *State Register* assessed what had happened, "The Supreme Court of the United States, the highest and most dignified tribunal in any civilized country, and composed of the very first order of talent in the world, and to whose decisions it is an honor to bow with respectful deference, have had the darling bantling of black republicanism under consideration, and announce it illegitimate. They say it is the offspring of red hot abolitionism, and cannot be acknowledged as having anything honest or upright about it."

In the South, the decision was praised everywhere. On March 10, the Memphis *Appeal* assured readers that "the constitutional rights of the South are thus vindicated . . . and enforced by the only tribunal which could settle the question permanently and satisfactorily to the great mass of the people." "This," the editor optimistically maintained, "will tranquilize the country." As for objections to the decision, they were dismissed as Black Republican–abolitionist assaults on the Constitution, similar to their assaults on the Bible. Over the next two weeks, the *Appeal* carried editorials denouncing Republican newspapers for their attacks on the Court, the decision, and the South in general. The editor declared the Republican press to have "erected a despotism of opinion in the northern states by which they mean to sacrifice every other great interest of the country. They have failed to win over the public but refuse to accept the failure."[15]

In New Orleans, the *Crescent*'s editor dismissed opposition to the decision and denunciation of the Court as an indication of the true character of Black Republicans.[16] In South Carolina the Charleston *Mercury* used the decision to chide people of its own region who had accused it of taking extremist positions. The editor announced proudly that the decision proved that "we have simply been a step in advance of the highest tribunal in the country, in declaring what was the law of the land and seeking honestly and faithfully to enforce it."[17] The *Mercury*'s editor described the great success of the southern people notwithstanding northerners' long history of hostility toward the South and its interests. With the decision in hand, the newspaper insisted that it was time for southern politicians to stop playing politics and unite in defense of the South.

In Virginia, the influential Richmond *Enquirer* editorialized at length on March 13 about the *Dred Scott* decision. It used the case as a means of addressing the entire history of the growing agitation over slavery and pleaded with northerners to leave southerners alone. It concluded, however, with fears that the fanaticism of abolitionists would not abate and that southerners, as fire-eaters provoked northerners and led them to express hatred of the South, would respond with hatred of all northerners because of the "fanatics'" provocations. In an editorial replete with rhetorical passion the *Enquirer* issued a warning to northerners:

> If the people of the North would cease to hurl thunderbolts at us from their pulpits, to fulminate firebrands into our society through their press, to attempt to intercept us in every territory, to defraud and to force us out of our rights; if in other words, they would render unto Caesar the things that are Caesar's; concede to us equality in the Union, offer no illegal and unjust obstruction to the extension of our institutions, if they would *let us alone* and leave slavery to the states, and to the same protection and privileges enjoyed by all other property under the Constitution, the *agitation* of the question would come to an end on the instant. The trouble would cease simultaneously with the cause that produced it. But, as long as they empty their vials of wrath upon our heads, ours must be emptied on theirs. If they propagate calumnies, we must refute them. If they incite *their* people to hate and assault the South, we must incite *our* people to *reciprocate the hatred,* and repel the attacks. If they smite us on the cheek, we cannot and will not turn the other to them too. If there is a danger in agitation, there is still more danger in supineness and submission.

The editor concluded this summary of where things stood between the sections by assuring readers that the South took a defensive position. It was the southerners who were wronged. It was they who were accused of immorality. It was their institutions that were challenged. "We leave their [the North's] domestic matters to themselves," he advised, "and all we ask is an observance on their part of the same policy towards us." The *Enquirer* called upon southerners to defend themselves, declaring that the South would be ready as long as the North seemed poised to fight. "As long as *their* sword is unsheathed, ours will [be] also."

So much for Taney's hope that the *Dred Scott* decision would bring closure to disputes over slavery. Portrayals of "barbarous people" acting without a sense of honor, ignoring the law whenever it suited them, risking the American heritage and the Republic for the sake of their own selfish interests, and creating anarchy when order was so necessary to society's well-being surfaced again in newspapers north and south. These were all images that had been so evident after the Brooks-Sumner incident and were reappearing in the American press in the aftermath of the *Dred Scott* decision. As in the case of the Brooks-Sumner incident, the characterization of the villains of the piece was in the eye of the beholder. In that incident the issue was often reduced to the dangers of rejecting the law and the mores of civilized society. In the *Dred Scott* case it was on one side the appearance of a partisan interpretation of the law and on the other the seeming refusal of an element of the society to obey the law.

People in each region were questioning the honor of those in the other, doubting their willingness to obey the law, and fearing that majority rule would be set aside or that majority rule would be allowed to deny the minority their legitimate rights under the Constitution. To people north and south, Democrat and Republican, what the debate over slavery demonstrated was the urgent need to protect the legacy of the Founders and preserve the Republic.

Taney, Bennett, and many others, north and south, hoped that with the Court's decision in hand, and with the old Jacksonian James Buchanan in the White House, calm would be restored to the country. Nevertheless, what the Richmond *Enquirer* labeled the "agitation" continued and intensified. In December 1857 another episode began that heightened anxiety regarding the future of the Republic. That was the attempt by southern politicians in the federal government, with the support of the president and some northern Democrats, to resolve the all too often violent dispute over the status of slavery in the Kansas Territory and, as in the *Dred Scott* case, to find a solution that would please southerners. Once again, efforts to stop the conflict resulted in inflaming passions and heightening controversy, and once again the press's use of extreme language and pejorative explanations of events both reflected and influenced public sentiments and worked to make matters worse.

4   Kansas and the Lecompton Constitution: Does the Majority Rule?

In the months that followed the *Dred Scott* decision, press attention turned back to the conflicts in Kansas. Political center stage was seized by maneuvering in Kansas Territory by advocates from each side of the slavery debate, first to gain dominance in the territorial legislature and then to control the choice of delegates to the state constitutional convention. Then, because each side created its own territorial government, each had its own constitutional convention and wrote a proposed constitution. Finally, in the winter of 1857–58, attention shifted to Washington, where Congress and the president had to decide for Kansas whether its constitution would be slave or free.

This state constitutional dispute marked the beginning of the unraveling of America's only remaining important national political party. As Chief Justice Roger Taney had hoped in vain that *Dred Scott* would quiet the furor, Sen. Stephen Douglas had hoped that his Kansas-Nebraska Act, based on the principle of popular sovereignty, would solve the festering issue. The old jurist and the ambitious politician were both dead wrong.

Proponents of the Kansas-Nebraska Act insisted that there was no more democratic way in which to resolve the question of slavery in a territory than to let the majority determine it. What they did not recognize was how difficult it would be to determine the will of a majority. Failure to resolve the issue caused the disputants to become increasingly more shrill. In all the years of conflict in the Kansas Territory, nothing contributed more to sectional anger and political division than what appeared to be the principle of majority rule. Each side accused the other of deception in their respective efforts to determine the will of the majority, a keystone of republican principles.[1] To quote the New York *Herald,* Kansas was the "apple of discord," and both sides took large bites of that apple.[2]

The violent incidents that led both newspaper editors and politicians to label the territory "bleeding Kansas" certainly contributed to the climate of fear and mutual recrimination that increasingly characterized the public mood during the decade. Although the press duly reported and explained each of these incidents in its own way, violence in Kansas and other territories was long-standing. Although it was deplored, it was also expected.[3]

It was the difficulty of determining the will of the majority, not violent incidents, that made the situation in Kansas so volatile. As Kansas moved toward statehood the election of delegates to a constitutional convention that would produce the required state constitution provided a focal point for the debate over how to find the will of the majority. It was in that constitution that the legality or illegality of slavery would be determined. Thus, the Kansas debate was not about the good or evil of slavery, it was about whether the majority should govern and who constituted the majority.

When the Douglas-led Democrats passed the Kansas-Nebraska Act, the obvious agenda that produced the political compromise necessary for passage was the understanding that Nebraska's people would approve a state constitution that prohibited slavery in the state-to-be while Kansans would approve a constitution that permitted slavery. That presented a practical dilemma, first to President Franklin Pierce and then to President James Buchanan: The majority of settlers in Kansas were not slaveholders, and most of them saw slavery as a threat to their economic well-being. Indeed, virtually no one in Kansas owned a slave, even though a significant minority of the population had moved there from slave states. Democratic Party politicians and the newspaper editors who supported them feared that support for the principle of popular sovereignty, should Kansas settlers vote to exclude slavery, would be greatly diminished and the slavery issue would rise to the fore again, splintering the party.

The succession of Kansas territorial governors each in turn faced an impossible task. Both the president who appointed them and the party that controlled the Congress expected them to employ the principle of popular sovereignty while at the same time producing a proslavery result. Those governors, and the federal troops under their jurisdiction, had to deal with vigilante activities from advocates on both sides of the slavery issue. This raised questions that were very difficult to answer. Who should the soldiers protect, who should they arrest, who should territorial judges try, and, finally (and most troubling), who constituted the legitimate citizens of the territory? No matter what federal officials in the territory did, they were bound to displease a segment of the Kansas population as well as one or another of the most powerful political interests in the federal capital.

With more than the necessary population to qualify, and with a territorial government unable to establish and keep order, both sides pressed for statehood. Whether Kansas would become a free state or a slave state would be determined in a territorial constitutional convention. Yet the fair election of a generally agreed upon group of legitimate delegates, given the political climates in both Kansas and Washington, could not be accomplished. Faced with what they believed to be a rigged election, antislavery advocates—"free-soilers"— boycotted the process and proceeded to elect their own slate of delegates.

Kansans thus found themselves with two slates of delegates to two constitutional conventions, each of which produced a proposed constitution. One allowed slavery, and the other prohibited it. Senator Douglas protested that the principle of popular sovereignty had been violated. But President Buchanan, convinced of the need to satisfy the demands of southerners in his party, endorsed the proslavery Lecompton Constitution (named for the town in which the constitutional convention had been held). The Lecompton document then was submitted to Congress for ratification.

Throughout the fall and winter of 1857–58 Congress debated whether to ratify the Lecompton Constitution and admit Kansas as a slave state. Ultimately, Congress voted it down, thus leaving Kansas a territory. Federal legislators argued not about whether slavery was right or wrong but about the way in which the will of the majority had been determined. Although some northerners considered the proposed constitution to be contrary to the will of the majority in Kansas, many northern Democrats and most southerners, regardless of party, continued to support the Lecompton Constitution, even after Congress had rejected it. When the vote went against them, they charged that Congress had denied the will of the majority and undermined the rule of law. The issues emanating from the Lecompton Constitution debate would divide the Democratic Party and, more definitively than at any prior time, push American politics toward political allegiance based on the section of the country in which one lived rather than on traditional party loyalty.

On December 14, 1857, the New Orleans *Crescent* editorialized about the Lecompton debate with particular reference to Douglas's attacks on the Buchanan administration for having endorsed the Lecompton document. The *Crescent* insisted that Douglas's actions "show how the political winds blow Northward." To those who held more moderate views and had hopes that northern business interests would never risk the Union for the sake of ending slavery, the newspaper argued that the moderates should "come to terms with the facts—demagogues in the North will betray them." On December 21, the *Crescent*'s editor, after continuing his attack on Douglas and predicting that "the Kansas game of fraud and deception upon the people of the South is pretty nearly played out," called for the South to unite politically against the North. The common enemy for southerners was the "abolition fanaticism" that the newspaper claimed now controlled northern public opinion.

December 21, 1857, was the day of the scheduled vote in the U.S. Senate on the constitution, and after reminding readers of how vitally important that decision was, the *Crescent* argued, "If it is approved it will force the North to respect the Constitutional rights of the South or if not [approved] will divide the Union." Anticipating the worst, the editor warned of "the spirit of envenomed hostility which animates the masses of the northern people towards the southern people." These northerners would deny southern people their rights, attack their honor, and undermine their interests. The editorial concluded, "We are weary of this eternal slavery agitation which has entailed nothing but loss, persecution and contumely upon the South."

Five days later, on December 26, with Congress having rejected the Lecompton Constitution, the *Crescent* lamented the "treachery" evident in the vote and criticized any southerner who called for peace. Soon after that the newspaper warned that in the wake of the Lecompton defeat they must ask "will they live or die as freemen or will they consent to exist in and occupy a lower position?" In effect, would southerners become like their own slaves? The *Crescent* insisted that the entire crisis was the result of northern desire to interfere with slavery and that it marked the end of any chance for future slave states to enter the Union. The *Crescent* laid out the drama. The conflict in Kansas, it made clear, was about northerners seeking to dominate southerners and about southern loss of rights and honor; it rang the death knell for any future expansion of slavery. The newspaper sought to convince its audience that the tide of northern political power would roll over the South.

In Memphis, the *Appeal,* after publishing the details of the Lecompton Constitution, supported President Buchanan's stand in favor of the document. The newspaper optimistically predicted that approving the document would bring the conflict in Kansas to an end, leaving its people to decide the issues that divided them.[4] Two days later, with Douglas's opposition to the constitution on record and while maintaining its firm support for Lecompton, the *Appeal* used more dramatic terms to portray the threat to the South if the constitution were defeated. On December 16 the editor accused those who opposed ratification of being "unpatriotic," and he warned all northerners, especially northern Democrats, that the South would be united on the issue.

On the day of the vote in the Senate, the newspaper lashed out at Stephen Douglas, declaring him the Democratic Party's "fallen star" and likening him to both Martin Van Buren, who in 1848 deserted the Democratic Party, and Thomas Hart Benton, the Democratic senator from Missouri who also opposed the Lecompton Constitution and by so doing contributed to the division of the Democratic Party.[5] Like the New Orleans *Crescent,* the *Appeal* asserted that Douglas and those Democrats in Congress who agreed with him had sold out the South. The publications turned on him vehemently; the *Appeal* went as far as to label the Illinois senator a "leader of the Black Republicans."[6]

Farther North, the Lecompton issue resulted in a serious fissure in the ranks of the Democratic Party and in the Democratic press. In Cincinnati, the southern-sympathizing *Enquirer* lashed out at Douglas and praised Buchanan. In the wake of the defeat of the Lecompton Constitution, and in an effort to minimize the damage to the party, the newspaper insisted that the Democratic president and the powerful Illinois senator differed over tactics rather than over the legitimacy of the popular-sovereignty principle.[7] The *Enquirer* urged Democrats to stop quarreling among themselves and to focus their anger on the free-soilers in Kansas and in the Congress.

On December 29, 1857, faced with defeat of the Lecompton Constitution in Congress, the newspaper editorialized again on the subject, now arguing that the principle of popular sovereignty was that the people of a territory should decide the issue of slavery and that Congress, once the people acted, should have no further say in the matter. A day later, the *Enquirer* warned readers that the free-soilers' boycott of the Lecompton convention was part of a grand conspiracy on the part of Black Republicans. The editor carried the conspiracy theory to the point of arguing that Republicans liked having the issue of "bleeding Kansas" and thus had plotted to make Kansas a slave state in order to keep the issue alive.

In Washington, D.C., the *Evening Star* accused Douglas of splitting the Democratic Party. Like the *Appeal,* the *Star* noted the similarity between Martin Van Buren's desertion of the party in 1848 and Stephen Douglas's current action.[8] On January 4, 1858, the *Star* again attacked Douglas, characterizing his actions as arising from his presidential ambitions. Only such ambition could explain why he had become an advocate "of the doctrine that the laws should not be enforced at all hazards, because a party in the Territory proclaim themselves above them, of the legality of which said laws, but yesterday as it were, there was no more earnest open and vehement defender than himself." The *Star* assured readers that no southern publication supported Douglas.

"Why do we quarrel so much over niggers or no niggers in far away Kansas?" asked James Gordon Bennett of New York *Herald* readers two days after the vote, recognizing the difficulty the Lecompton Constitution issue posed for Democrats.[9] A few days later, Bennett warned that "the Democratic party [is] on the verge of dissolution" and declared these to be "the last days of the party as Jackson created it," that is, a coalition of northerners and southerners.[10]

The *Missouri Democrat* in St. Louis, an ardent supporter of Thomas Hart Benton against his Missouri Democratic enemy, the proslavery David Atchison, defended Douglas. In an editorial on December 2, 1857, the *Democrat* insisted that "in determining a Constitution for Kansas the slavery people will not allow the people to decide." The newspaper accused proslavery forces of "trying to get Congress to force a pro-slavery Constitution on the people of Kansas" and called on northern Democrats not to let that happen. In a provocative statement the next day, the newspaper declared "all the power on earth could never enforce such a tyrannical code upon the people of any state. *The men of Kansas denied the ballot box will resort to the bayonet.* And they will do *right.*"

In a December 5 editorial, the *Democrat* continued to describe and dramatize the dispute over the Lecompton Constitution: "The issue is whether or not people are willing to abandon the cause of free labor—whether, in short, the rights of white men and free men are to be eternally prostrated before the clamorous impudence of a few aristocratic planters and the hungry cry of a batch of impoverished office seekers, whose Tory pedigree is their only claim to notoriety." The editorial concluded with the declaration that the "whole issue is whether the will of the people will be obeyed."

Nine days later, on December 14, with the vote in Congress still a week away, the *Missouri Democrat* attacked James Buchanan for supporting a "bogus Constitution" in Kansas and warned all concerned that the Lecompton Constitution would "prove the inciting cause to an amount of sectional ill-feeling and excitement to which its experience as a territory furnished no parallel." Although southern newspapers saw the Lecompton Constitution as a solution to the Kansas difficulties, the *Democrat* and all Republican newspapers viewed it as the opposite. The editorial concluded with another burst of extreme language: "It promises to blow the National Democracy into fragments, and hurl from place and power the present rulers of the country, at Washington, who are too gross and too dishonest to breathe the atmosphere which has been rendered pure by the presence of a Washington, a Jefferson, and a Jackson."

In the days that followed, the St. Louis newspaper kept up its attack on "the bogus Constitution" and all who supported it, insisting that they were ignoring the rights and will of the people. Four days after the vote that assured that Congress would not approve the document, the *Democrat* demanded that the administration act on the "basis of principle and not expediency. There is no middle ground."[11] But if there were no middle ground, and principle—not expediency—must dictate action, what, given the clash of principles, would be the consequences for Kansas, the Democratic Party, and the Union? In the winter of 1858 most newspapers from all regions of the country and the representatives of major political parties left that question unanswered. Over time, answers began to be suggested, and for some newspapers in the South, such as the New Orleans *Crescent,* the conclusion was obvious—disunion. The possibility of secession produced varying responses from the northern press of each party.

Like James Gordon Bennett, John Forney, editor of the *Press,* a Democratic Philadelphia-published newspaper, saw Kansas, especially the Lecompton Constitution issue, as damaging both to the Democratic Party and to the country. After praising Stephen Douglas, Forney insisted that the key premise of the Kansas-Nebraska Act had been majority rule. The editor denounced southern newspapers for attacking Douglas and for "clamoring for minority rule in Kansas."[12] Forney cautioned southerners not to think that the North would give in to their every demand, especially not a demand that involved the most fundamental principle of republican government, majority rule.

As a staunch Democrat, Forney wanted to turn his readers' attention away from the Kansas dispute. "Why," he asked, "make the fundamental rights of *free white men* subordinate to the rights of a few miserable negroes? Is the chief end of a State Government to hold or not to hold negro slaves?"[13] The editor went on to insist that the Kansas Constitution and the election of constitutional convention delegates that preceded it were the key tests of the Kansas-Nebraska Act. All would be well if elections were fair and majority rule was the order of the day.

The next day, December 17, the *Press* again editorialized about Lecompton. This time it was a plea to southerners ("our brothers and our co-partners") not to be misled by sectional leaders. Readers were reminded of how men of both sections had fought together in the Revolution and joined in support of Washington's administration. Forney declared the Lecompton Constitution to be "a false principle" despite attempts by sectional leaders to persuade them that it was a true one. Minority will over the majority was intolerable, and if southerners were to allow sectional passions to dominate they would fall into the hands of "fanatics." The editor urged southerners to recognize that those who opposed the Lecompton Constitution were not enemies of the South, nor did they wish to end slavery. Rather, they were defending a basic principle of republican government, majority rule, a "principle that protects all." Forney concluded the piece by reminding readers that "this principle of majority rule was what the fathers fought the Revolution to defend." Here was another case of invoking the republican heritage and the need to protect that heritage as the key challenge of the time.

As the Lecompton Constitution issue lingered in legislative halls during the weeks and months that followed, the *Press* continued to tell the South in blunt terms that it could not expect northerners to support "what is unjust." On January 1, 1858, it argued that, contrary to claims of southern newspapers and some northern Democratic ones that supported the Lecompton Constitution, if that constitution were ever adopted it would lead not to peace in Kansas but to war. The *Press* warned that a civil war in Kansas would spread to neighboring states and territories. In his harshest condemnation yet of the role of southerners in the Kansas dispute, Forney insisted that some in the South (a "grand conspiracy") were determined to destroy the Union. On January 9, 1858, the Philadelphia editor defended the Kansas-Nebraska Act as the Democrats' way of stopping "a sectional war against the South by abolitionists," whom the editor labeled as fanatics. By mid-February the *Press* was more dubious: "We begin to doubt whether, indeed, this is a land of liberty and law." It also decried "the miserable handful of discontents in the South."[14]

Northern Democrats faced a serious dilemma in trying to keep their party together. On the one hand, they saw danger in endorsing what many northerners believed to be an illegal constitution proposed by a fraudulently elected group of men and reflecting the interests of a minority of citizens. On the other hand, there was peril in seeming to be on the side of free-soilers and abolitionists, who were the South's enemies and the Republican Party's friends. The Lecompton Constitution, especially Douglas's rejection of it, greatly weakened the Democratic Party. It also destroyed any chance Douglas might have had as a presidential candidate to represent both sections of the party in a future national election.

For Republicans, the response to the Lecompton Constitution posed no dilemma. The proposed constitution seemed a perfect issue to attract and unite adherents to the new party. Republican newspapers opposed it in the name of defending the Republic and its principle of majority rule. There was no need to argue over the controversial issue of slavery when the issue of preserving republican principles was available.

In a December 23 editorial the Republican Indianapolis *Journal* sounded the battle cry: "The only issue in Kansas today is that of self-government not slavery or free labor. And if the government would act in good faith to their profession, and carry out the only true principles of free government, viz.

permitting the majority to rule, there would be 'peace in Kansas' from that hour forth. But that policy is ignored by a pro slavery administration [the federal government]."

The *Journal* labeled the proposed Kansas constitution both "the Lecompton swindle" and "a notorious fraud."[15] In the days immediately after the first vote in Congress on the Lecompton Constitution, the newspaper attributed great and evil power to Democratic newspapers. The editor accused those supporting the Lecompton Constitution of "turning traitors to free government and endorsing despotism." He also warned the Buchanan administration and its supporters that "the Administration never existed that could face the people of this Union, after creating a civil war to compel a majority to submit to a minority."[16]

The Republican Chicago *Tribune* referred to the delegates to the Lecompton convention as "felons." Although agreeing with Douglas that what was needed in Kansas was a free election, the newspaper was not about to join hands with the Illinois senator of the opposing party. The *Tribune,* in a December 17 editorial, dismissed Douglas's popular-sovereignty theory as "humbug" and on December 19 attacked him, claiming that his break with Buchanan on the Lecompton issue was a "sham." Douglas, the newspaper maintained, "has been the defender and approver of a whole series of outrages perpetrated in Kansas." Moreover, "His masters are the slave drivers," and he had approved of the *Dred Scott* decision.[17]

Greeley's New York *Tribune* took the stand that the principle of popular sovereignty was a worthy one if followed honestly. But the newspaper labeled as "fraud" the process that produced the Lecompton Constitution. The *Tribune* warned that southern members of Congress who were trying to force this proposed constitution, which was the product of illegal actions and reflective of a minority of the people involved, were playing "a deep and dangerous game."[18] They were "aiming at a dissolution of the Union and the Formation of a pure Slaveholding Republic," and the editor accused the culprits of wanting to drive free states, or at least most of them, out of the Union. If the Republicans won the 1860 presidential election, the piece predicted, those southerners would resort to force.

Well aware that the Douglas-Buchanan split was hurting the Democratic Party and helping the Republicans, the New York newspaper, like its Chicago namesake, gave much space to detailing Douglas's opposition to the constitution without embracing the Illinois senator himself. In a December 29 editorial, the *Tribune* attacked Douglas's motives for opposing the Lecompton Constitution, ascribing to him only political concerns and not principle. The newspaper insisted that Douglas opposed the Lecompton Constitution "because he fears it will wreck the Democratic Party." Indeed, the New York *Tribune* argued that it was Douglas's popular-sovereignty theory, embodied in the Kansas-Nebraska Act, which he took credit for passing, that was the cause of all the trouble in Kansas.

As with the Brooks-Sumner incident and the *Dred Scott* decision, the Kansas conflict, in particular the Lecompton Constitution debate, provided concrete proof of two general propositions regarding the northern press's portrayal of southern society and itself. One was a growing sense that southerners, infected by or obsessed by the institution of slavery and all that institution implied, were incapable of civilized behavior. Readers of Republican newspapers were presented with the view of a southern world in which murder and mayhem were common occurrences. Such behavior was left unpunished and even condoned. The South was to be perceived as a society governed by an aristocracy and characterized by a total lack of regard for obedience to law or respect for the rights of others. In such a society, republican principles would be—indeed, were being—ignored, put aside in the face of a crude embracing of self-interest. As that press described and explained them, the Brooks-Sumner incident, the *Dred Scott* decision, and the Lecompton Constitution each provided concrete and dramatic evidence of the validity of those generalizations.

The second general proposition put forward by some northern newspapers centered on the obligation of northern society to defend civilized behavior and insist on obedience to the law. By so doing, society would preserve the heritage of the Founding Fathers and the Republic and all for which it stood. While denouncing the words and deeds of abolitionists, who in their religious fanaticism might sacrifice the sacred Republic for the sake of an inferior people (blacks), northern newspapers insisted that their readers behave like civilized, law-abiding whites whose interest was in promoting the society that had been bequeathed to them. In their portrayal of the Brooks-Sumner incident, the *Dred Scott* decision, and the Lecompton Constitution, the Republican press challenged northerners to meet those sacred obligations.

The southern press also invoked the need to defend the republican heritage. That press portrayed southerners as the true heirs to what Washington, Jefferson, and Jackson, each a slaveholder, had fought so valiantly to achieve. Those southerners must have wondered how anyone could think that owning slaves was somehow antithetical to being devoted to the Republic. They saw no contradiction between slavery and republicanism. The Republic, they argued, was threatened but not by them. The threat instead came from those in the North—"fanatics," "abolitionists," and "puritans" (all terms that appeared often in the southern press)—who cared not for the Republic but rather for the imposition of what they defined to be virtue and what they interpreted to be the will of God. They would root out evil, as they defined it, at any cost. Northern fanatics considered the Republic, the Constitution, law, order, and the well-being of the white race unimportant if those principles of republican society stood in the way of carrying out their abolitionist agenda.

Newspapers did much to give life to conflicting views on the part of those of each section regarding those of the other. As the press described them, these events provided evidence that in the public mind, slavery, pro or con, was the cause of one part of American society believing the other to be diseased. It was the effect of each society's view of the other as diseased that led to the belief that each society had abandoned the faith of the Founders. When they discussed the Kansas trouble, neither southern nor northern newspapers spent time debating the virtues or vices of slavery. Yet it was slavery or opposition to it that defined the character of those people, and the future of the Republic depended on the character of its people. Each side saw in these incidents evidence of fatal character flaws and a loss of virtue.

Then, between October 17 and 20, 1859, reports of an effort, led by a white man, to provoke a slave rebellion in the South appeared in newspapers across the country. In its wake the rhetorical lines of battle became sharper, the intemperance reflected in the press's language more vivid, and the verbal portraits of the good or evil of the key characters were dramatized even more. John Brown and his men provided a drama that surpassed earlier controversies. His actions, plans, and expectations as well as his treatment once captured preoccupied the mass media from the day of the attack to the day Brown and some of his band of conspirators were hanged.

5　John Brown's Raid:
Violence in a Republican Society

It was May 1858 before a compromise bill on the disposition of the Kansas constitution finally passed both houses of Congress. The bill called for a referendum in Kansas to determine the fate of the proposed state constitution. In August 1858 an overwhelming majority defeated the constitution. Kansas remained a territory until January 1861, when, with a number of slave states no longer represented in Congress, an antislavery constitution was approved. The conflicts in Kansas had divided Democrats, further splintering the country along sectional lines. For some deeply involved in the conflicts and violence in Kansas there were wounds that would not heal.

The defeat of the Lecompton Constitution left Kansas a territory populated by settlers who were traumatized by vigilantes. Whether they actually had experienced or had been threatened by vigilante-provoked violence or had merely heard of it, that brand of so-called justice was frighteningly real. The American public saw the territory's history as one marked by burning, looting, and killing. Among the victims and instigators of such crimes were John Brown and his family. In retaliation against the loss of one of his sons at the hands of proslavery men, Brown participated in the killing of several proslavery settlers at Potawatomie Creek in southeastern Kansas. His role in this incident earned him the label "Potawatomie Brown."

The story of what happened at that small creek found its way into the eastern press, both North and South, but only as one of the many accounts of violence in the Kansas Territory. Had John Brown stayed in Kansas it is likely that he would have gone relatively unnoticed either then or thereafter. But Brown would make his mark not in Kansas but in Virginia. What happened in Virginia proved that Brown was more than a free-soiler determined to keep slaveholders and their slaves out of Kansas. He believed himself to be God's instrument in leading a crusade to end slavery, and the press, whether friendly or unfriendly toward him, conveyed that belief to readers. Although Brown had played only a minor role in the effort to keep slavery out of Kansas and the Harpers Ferry, Virginia, raid failed in its goal of provoking a slave rebellion, his actions, his trial, and his execution were important.[1] To northerners and southerners alike, Brown became a dramatic symbol of the Republic's ills and uncertain future.

During 1858 and well into 1859, taking advantage of his friendship with the wealthy New York philanthropist and abolitionist Gerrit Smith, Brown made several train trips east to meet with abolitionists who might assist him in his cause. Just how much of his plan Brown revealed to those abolitionists has remained a mystery, but we do know that he sought and received money from several of them, including Smith. With those funds he rented a farmhouse near Harpers Ferry, Virginia, a town on the Potomac River in northwestern Virginia, some ninety miles from Richmond and Washington and connected by rail to both cities. He also ordered a large number of spikes from a manufacturer in Connecticut, to be used by slaves as weapons, and in time brought several men from Kansas and elsewhere, including one of his sons, to Virginia. His plan was to seize a federal arsenal located in that village, take the arms stored there, and distribute them to slaves. Once armed, he would lead those slaves in an uprising against their masters. Brown believed that as word of the rebellion spread a slave insurrection would engulf the South.

On the morning of October 17, 1859, the telegraph wire services began to receive reports that they passed on to their newspaper clients. A violent conflict had occurred the day before in the town of Harpers Ferry. Details were sketchy. Newspapers were uncertain about who had initiated the violence and why. Some accounts reported that as many as seven to eight hundred workers, angry over pay and working conditions at a local construction site, had attacked the town's citizenry. Others declared the event to be a massive uprising of slaves, a servile insurrection. Men had been shot and killed, but how many was also unclear.

By October 18 the details about what had happened became known and were communicated over the telegraph. In another day or two newspapers in all parts of the country were telling readers about John Brown, late of Kansas, who with a small band of white men and a few free blacks had assaulted the federal arsenal located in Harpers Ferry. Having neglected to cut the telegraph line out of Harpers Ferry, the attackers soon had to face a company of federal troops commanded by Col. Robert E. Lee. Brown and his men barricaded themselves inside the arsenal. Lee's men stormed it, killing several of the small band and wounding and capturing Brown and the others.[2]

Newspapers everywhere soon carried story after story about the raid and the discovery of what to some appeared to be evidence that Brown and his men were part of a wider conspiracy. When Virginia authorities searched the rented farmhouse that Brown used as a staging area, they found letters from a number of well-known northerners. There was proof that Brown had been in touch with the fugitive slave and abolitionist Frederick Douglass. Also among his correspondents was the noted Boston Unitarian minister Theodore Parker, who had been involved some years before in the attempt to free Anthony Burns, an accused runaway slave. Parker and others had used force to keep Burns out of the hands of slave-catchers, thus defying the Fugitive Slave Act. There were also letters from others sympathetic to abolitionists, including some members of Congress.

Fearful of arrest as a part of this alleged conspiracy, Frederick Douglass fled to Canada. Parker was already in Italy, seeking to recover his health, and died there soon after. Greatly agitated by his involvement with Brown and alleged support of the raid, Gerrit Smith suffered a nervous breakdown. There were no explicit references in the letters to the planned raid, and all of Brown's correspondents denied knowledge of his intention to attack the arsenal. Brown's raid conjured up images in southern minds of the Nat Turner rebellion in 1831, the slave uprising in Santo Domingo some thirty years before that, and all the other slave insurrections or rumors of such that had for decades circulated through southern society.

Both northern and southern newspapers referred to John Brown's "Quixotic" act. The raid on the Harpers Ferry arsenal brought northerners and southerners, Republicans and Democrats, face to face with the slavery issue in new and frightening ways. The drama of the north-south conflict became more intense than ever before, and the press of both regions added greatly to that drama. Newspapers that had been urging that the slavery issue be set aside and new compromises be found became even more hard-pressed than before to win over readers. It was hard to be neutral when writing and reading about John Brown and his men and the supposed conspiracy of which they may have been a part. Southern newspapers and most northern Democratic ones tied Brown's actions directly to abolitionists, who, in turn, were linked to Republicans. In the pages of those newspapers, what Brown did proved that, should Republicans gain political control of the country, the South could expect far more than a legislative assault on slavery. Servile insurrection, race war, and general anarchy were all part of what that segment of the press thought the Harpers Ferry raid augured for the future of the South. For their part, Republican editors, while decrying Brown's act, blamed his "mad" scheme on slave-holders who had driven him insane by their violent acts. They also denied any link between Brown, abolitionists, and the Republican Party.

Newspapers wrote the story in different ways, provided different versions of events, and offered different characterizations of the key figure, John Brown. For six weeks after the raid, until December 2, 1859, the day on which Brown was hanged by Virginia authorities, the story was rarely out of the daily newspapers. The press told the tale, interpreted the motives of the key actors, and provided the lessons to be learned, both shaping and reflecting what was in readers' minds.

Of course, story, interpretation, and lesson all differed from newspaper to newspaper. Region and politics shaped each differing version of "reality." What the Harpers Ferry incident demonstrated about the attitudes of people in all parts of the country was that each group feared the other, that fear prompted anger and hostility, and that the press's use of language and interpretation of events and the motives of key actors brought those attitudes and emotions to the surface. Only the presence of irrational fear could explain how such a wild and impractical action could produce such an overreaction to it. As was the case with the *Dred Scott* decision and the debate over the Lecompton Constitution, Harpers Ferry raised political decibel levels and temperatures on both sides of the Mason-Dixon line.

In its October 31 edition the always cautious Washington, D.C., *National Intelligencer* remarked on the way in which Brown's attack had pushed the slavery issue to the fore and revealed how truly deep the antagonisms on the subject went. The editor declared it "time to resolve the slavery controversy. It has been a grand error to make it a stalking horse for political leaders, and the sooner the country learns to retrace its steps and settle down into the old paths where the compact of the Constitution leads us, the better it will be for the pace of the country and for that harmonious working of the Union, which has only been disturbed by breaking away from its original boundaries."

For the *Intelligencer,* still living up to its nameplate motto of "liberty and union," the hope that such an extreme and dramatic act would arouse people to the danger of debating slavery was understandable. On November 12, 1859, after Brown and his surviving compatriots had been tried, found guilty, and sentenced by a Virginia court, the *Intelligencer* told readers about "the tragic scenes of which Harper's Ferry has been the theatre." The editor accused both politicians and newspapers of exploiting the episode for their own interests. Sharing its frustration, the newspaper warned, "The language of passionate and exaggerated complaint is ever sure to provide reaction on the part of those who are aware of its injustice, and in this way it is that opportunities of public pacification may become only the nurseries of fresh dissensions. When will the exponents of public opinion learn that the language of earnestness is always the language of moderation, and that dignified remonstrance affords a better proof of conscious resolve than words of rogue crimination?"

"The language of passionate and exaggerated complaint" indeed characterized the treatment of the incident on the part of southern and northern Democratic newspapers and, as the *Intelligencer* predicted, was countered in kind by Republican newspapers. The level of dissension was heightened, and the tone of newspaper language and imagery became more shrill.

If the Washington, D.C., *National Intelligencer* was restrained in its response to the raid, not so a rival, the *Evening Star.* In its first report of the attack on October 18, the day on which John Brown was wounded and captured, the *Star* labeled him one of those "freedom shriekers so long supported in their career of murder and rapine by money previously collected throughout the North at prayer meetings and on other such occasions."

Southern newspapers often portrayed northerners as religious fanatics, and the *Star* was no exception. It attributed to the attackers not some high-minded motive but rather described them as thieves seeking plunder. As the *Star* warned, "Thus have the people of the slaveholding states had the first taste of the ultimate ends of demagogues who lead in political abolitionism."[3] This was followed by the assertion that Republican newspapers, by their support of men such as Brown, had encouraged this action. As far as Democratic newspapers north and south were concerned, abolitionists were Republicans and Republicans were abolitionists. The *Star* and many other southern and pro-southern newspapers argued that the raid had proved the connection. To the Republican warnings of a slave-power conspiracy Democratic newspapers laid out the case for an abolitionist-Republican conspiracy.

In the days that followed, the *Star* built on its initial charge of conspiracy. In a piece published on October 22 it insisted that what had happened was the work "not by a few crazy fanatics, but by a powerful well organized party." The editor added that "the day is rapidly approaching when the slavery question will be settled one way or the other—either by dissolution of the Union or by a resolution of sentiment at the North, through which a conservative respect for the slavery compromises of the Constitution will again be in the ascendant there." In effect, the *Star* and many other southern newspapers told readers that what had happened at Harpers Ferry proved that fanatics were gaining control of northern minds and hearts and that only a revolution in northern thinking could alter the situation and quiet southern fears.

The Memphis *Appeal* described the raid as an example of "northern madness."[4] As for Brown, the newspaper noted that many northern papers described him as crazy. The *Appeal*'s editor, however, insisted that if indeed Brown was crazy, he was made so "by the teachings of abolitionists" and that the "only tendency of abolition theories is anarchy, bloodshed and confusion."[5] Like the Washington *Star,* the *Appeal* linked abolition to the Black Republicans. On November 10, after Brown's conviction, the newspaper warned that northerners must recognize "that feeling is growing in the South that the Union is not worth preserving. The North must reject the fanaticism and madness of abolitionists as shown at Harper Ferry." The editorial concluded with the demand that either the North get rid of the Black Republican Party or "there is little hope for the Union to exist."

Farther South, the New Orleans *Crescent* told readers that what happened at Harpers Ferry proved to those in the South who did not see abolition as a serious threat that they were wrong. Brown's attack showed "abolition to be a conspiracy with vast and powerful ramifications through many states" and involved "men of high standing" in the North.[6] Now advocating secession, the *Crescent* also demanded that the South leave the Union before "this abolitionist spirit destroys the South." In the days and weeks that followed, and after the discovery at the farmhouse of Brown's correspondence, the *Crescent,* along with many other southern newspapers, demanded that Gerritt Smith and the other "conspirators" be put on trial in their northern home states or, better still, be sent to Virginia to be tried. The newspaper insisted that failure to root out and punish all conspirators would serve as further proof that northerners, en masse, had acquiesced in Brown's actions if not openly supported them. Following Brown's conviction and then his hanging, the newspaper noted with disgust that northern publications described him as a martyr.[7]

Linking Republicans to abolitionists—and both to northerners in general—many southern newspapers held northern society responsible for Harpers Ferry and for the division of the country that they predicted would follow from it. The Nashville *Whig,* while denouncing Republicans, also found the incident a reason to attack the Democratic Party. No Tennessee Whig was going to find it easy to embrace the party of Andrew Jackson, as the newspaper reminded readers. If Democrats had stood by the Compromise of 1850, the product of the efforts of Henry Clay, that epitome of the old Whig Party, rather than promote the Kansas-Nebraska Act, the work of the northern Democrat Stephen Douglas, the debates over slavery would have been put to rest.[8] Having made that assertion, the newspaper called for the organization of a new national party, which "avoiding the sectional extremes of both [Republicans and Democrats], and studiously ignoring the slavery issue, shall assume the control of the Government on both national and conservative principles. . . . Such a party is the only hope of the nation, the only safe guard of our liberties, and the only surety for the restoration of peace and harmony. The friends of law and order, and the lovers of the Union, should devote themselves to the task of forming such a party."⁹ A year later those who agreed did form such a party, the Constitutional Union Party, with Tennessean and long-time Jackson and Democratic Party foe John Bell leading its ticket. In 1860 Bell carried the Upper South region of Virginia, Kentucky, and Tennessee.

But, at least in the South, calls for moderation and hopes of avoiding the subject of slavery were lost in the passionate, anti-northern, secessionist rhetoric that appeared in the great majority of the region's papers. On the day Brown was hanged, December 2, 1859, the Mobile, Alabama, *Register* urged readers to recognize that "if we of the South are wise, we shall have learned a lesson. . . . we shall prepare for the future and the approaching conflict shall find us in arms." The *Register*'s call for the development of a full-blown southern nation was typical of the rhetoric southerners were reading in their newspapers.

On the day after the execution, the Raleigh *Register,* although not quite ready to concede that division of the nation was inevitable, castigated northerners but hoped that with Brown gone "the excitement of the North will subside." That, the North Carolina editor acknowledged, given the character of northerners, was a faint hope, because "fanaticism in the North is rampant and overrides everything."¹⁰ The people of Boston, the account added, were in "mourning, fasting and prayer, over the condign [appropriate] punishment of a Negro stealer, murderer, and traitor, and from fifty pulpits the Praise-God Bare bones belched forth volumes of blasphemy and treason."

For the Richmond *Enquirer,* the only way that northerners could make amends for what had happened would be to go to the polls in 1860 and repudiate the Black Republicans. The newspaper warned its own readers, as well as those who often had the chance to read *Enquirer* editorials reprinted in northern publications, that the Republic faced its greatest crisis:

> The Harper's Ferry *invasion* has advanced the cause of Dissension, more than any other event that has happened since the formation of the Government; it has rallied to that standard men who formerly looked upon it with horror; it has revived, with ten fold strength, the desire of a Southern confederacy. The heretofore, most determined friends of the Union may now be heard saying, "if under the form of a Confederacy [the Union] our peace is disturbed, our State invaded, its peaceful citizens cruelly murdered, and all the horrors of servile war forced upon us, by those who should be our warmest friends; if the form of a confederacy is observed, but its spirit violated, *and the people of the North sustain the outrage, then let disunion come.*"¹¹

The newspaper declared Brown and those who conspired with him to be guilty of "treason." The use of that word suggested that although Brown and his cohort conspired against the South, their real enemy was the Republic. They were traitors to the United States. If the Republic were to dissolve, those fanatics would be responsible for its demise.

The southern press offered blanket condemnation of the North in the wake of what the Richmond *Enquirer* dramatically labeled the "invasion," meaning to conjure up the image of an abolitionist army descending on the South. Northern Democratic newspapers were equally aggressive and passionate in their editorials, but they aimed that passion at political and press enemies in the North. They were not about to join in a blanket condemnation of all northerners.

Until the day Brown was hanged a number of southern newspapers reported rumors of a massive abolitionist attack aimed at freeing him from prison. The southern press trumpeted the message of the Harpers Ferry raid as the most horrendous evidence of the actions of despicable white northerners and of the lengths to which they would go, the laws they would break, to end slavery. As southerners read about them, the raid and the conspiracy were portrayed as direct and serious assaults on the South and on the Republic.

On October 18, with Brown now in custody and identified, James Gordon Bennett's New York *Herald,* although it had no evidence to support the claim, erroneously reported that an insurrection of blacks had occurred at Harpers Ferry and that northern abolitionists were leading "an extensive Negro Conspiracy in Virginia and Maryland." The report concluded with a statement: "This is what abolitionists will bring us." The following day, in analyzing what it claimed had happened, the *Herald* told readers that they should expect everyone in the southern states "to be exasperated with all the slavery agitators in the North."

Bennett's newspaper included among those agitators both William Seward, at that time the likely Republican presidential nominee in 1860, and Stephen Douglas, who in 1860 would run as the presidential candidate of a splintered Democratic Party. Like some other Democratic newspaper editors, Bennett had written off Douglas after his split with Buchanan over the Lecompton Constitution. The *Herald* warned that what had happened at Harpers Ferry "proves the South is not safe from abolitionist conspirators."[12] Moreover, it joined the southern press in equating abolitionists with Black Republicans and vice versa. Bennett insisted that the raid was a preview of what would happen if Seward were elected president. The piece concluded with a reminder that the "welfare of the South is necessary to the welfare of the North." Two days later the *Herald* explained that what it labeled Brown's insane actions were the result of following "antislavery agitators" who "furnished the ideas upon which the minds of such inflammable and reckless fanatics. . . . take fire."[13]

In Philadelphia, John Forney, editor of the *Press,* was unwilling to endorse the southern press's claim that abolitionists had captured the allegiance of the northern public, although he denounced what Brown did and stood for. Forney insisted that *"there are only a few extremists in the North,"* and they "can never obtain a commanding or controlling influence."[14] The editor then warned that northern extremists would have even less influence if they were not witness to the words and deeds of southern extremists. He urged southerners to deny power to extremists in their midst. In an October 20 editorial, the newspaper rejected the claim that Brown was part of a widespread conspiracy and urged that "all Americans must fight to prevent slave insurrections." A week later, in assessing the outcomes of the raid, Forney noted that most Republicans had disavowed Brown and that they felt compelled "to suppress the fanatics in their ranks."[15] Southerners were urged to drop efforts underway among some of their politicians to reopen the slave trade. Forney warned that "however secure the South may be in the control of her present slave population she should consider with deep concern how her slaves can be managed if the flood-gates are opened for the ingress of the wild barbarians of Africa in countless thousands, and if a new element of future danger is thus introduced." Ten days later, while still addressing the source of the trouble, a scathing piece appeared in the *Press,* attacking President Buchanan for capitulating to southern extremists in the Kansas crisis. It concluded by damning the president as being no better than Brown: "If it was right in James Buchanan to force slavery upon a people [in Kansas], it was right in John Brown to force freedom upon the South."[16] Forney insisted that Buchanan had acted for political reasons, whereas Brown had acted from principle. The editor meant no praise of John Brown but was heaping scorn on the Pennsylvania man who was president. Other northern Democratic newspapers were less critical of the South and Buchanan.

On the day Brown was captured, the Cincinnati *Enquirer* declared the raid to be "an abolition movement and the first open attack by that class of citizens to free the slaves of the South by force and bloodshed." Moreover, it insisted, "The welfare of the whole white race is put at stake."[17] The next day, October 19, the newspaper attributed the raid to the Republican Party, in particular to William Seward. Consistent with the southern press, the *Enquirer* pointed out how the raid made clear what could and would happen if a "Republican-Abolitionist President were ever elected." If the country were to come to civil war, it would be because of the actions of Seward; Ohio's Republican senator Salmon Chase, who was one of Brown's correspondents; and others whom the *Enquirer* labeled abolitionists. A few days later, acknowledging that slavery was now the prime divisive issue, the newspaper argued that in contrast to hardworking, virtuous whites who could be trusted with liberty, "slaves don't understand or want liberty only a chance to be idle given his nature and instincts." The editor concluded that given "the nature of slaves—slavery isn't wrong."[18]

In Springfield, Illinois, the pro-Democratic *State Register,* in an October 20 editorial, struck the same notes as the Cincinnati newspaper. The *Register* identified the attackers' purpose to be "the uprising of the Negroes throughout the South, a servile war, and its consequences—murder, rapine and robbery." Having identified the attackers' purpose, the *Register* connected them to "ultra Abolitionism" and attributed their actions to the teachings of Seward and Lincoln. For this newspaper, Seward, the author of the phrase "the irrepressible conflict," and Lincoln, who said "that the Union cannot continue as the fathers made it—part slave and part free states," were the true culprits in the Harpers Ferry horror. The editor denounced the Republican leaders: "When such men, by specious demagoguism, in the name of freedom and liberty, daily labor to weaken the bonds of our glorious governmental fabric, the work of sages and patriots, threatens the holders of black men as slaves, is it to be wondered at that ignorant, unprincipled and reckless camp followers of the party for which these leaders speak, attempt, practically, to illustrate the doctrines which they preach, and in advocacy of which they seek to obtain control of the national government." The editorial next denounced all Black Republicans as men organized to "stir the southern slaves to bathe their hands in the blood of the whites of the South. Traitorous scoundrels, with white faces, but black hearts, lead them and the country is stunned with their deeds of infamy, treason and blood." Thus for the editor of this Illinois newspaper, the message to convey was the need of all white men, north and south, to stop evil whites who would prompt a race war for the sake of political gain.

What seemed to resonate with most people, whatever their region or politics, was that Brown had not simply threatened the South. Rather, what was at stake was the security and the well-being of all white Americans. What was at risk was the Republic, the heritage derived from the Founders, the present form of government that assured law and order, and the future prospects of the country. That theme could be found even in the pages of northern Republican newspapers but with a reversal of roles. In those publications, Brown's actions were described as having awakened Americans not to the barbaric, anarchical, character of abolitionists but to those characteristics as found in slaveholders.

The Harpers Ferry raid put the Republican press on the defensive. Their political opponents had lost no time in linking them to John Brown and hence to abolitionists. While insisting that they did not condone what the "crazy" man had done, labeling Brown as mad was the best way to argue that this was an isolated incident and not part of a calculated northern plan of attack on the South. The Republican press labored to turn Harpers Ferry to its advantage.

Two days after Brown's capture and identification, and in the face of biting denunciation of Republicans as the party responsible for the lawless raid on Harpers Ferry, the quick-minded Thurlow Weed took the offensive. In an editorial in his Albany, New York, *Evening Journal,* Weed linked slaveholders and the Democratic Party and denounced them for lying about the Republicans' role in the attack. He reminded readers that the Republican Party in "all its platforms and declarations, and the life-long action of its members, show[s] that it contemplates only legal, peaceful and constitutional measures—neither interfering with Slavery in the States, nor countenancing mob violence anywhere."[19] Hence, Weed insisted, Republicans would not and did not inspire John Brown to act as he did. Instead, "The Slave holders themselves," he said, "are continually putting the idea of insurrection into the heads of their chattels." Weed argued that slaveholders did that by telling slaves and everyone else that abolitionist Republicans were conspiring to free them and thus giving slaves the hope and expectation that they would be freed. If and when there was violence, it would be fomented, albeit unwittingly, by slaveholders. As for Brown's actions, they were his reaction to the crimes of slaveholders in Kansas and "the Democratic Administration in Washington!" They had turned Brown into a "monomaniac."

Weed wrote on the day before Brown was to be executed that already the "muttered thunder of a pent-up sympathy is heard. . . . should John Brown be hung, the feeling will be augmented a hundred fold; and hatred of Slavery will become the predominant emotion in the breasts of millions who have thus far had neither fellowship nor sympathy with those who seek to goad the South into just such exhibitions of weakness and folly as these executions will afford."[20] So Weed predicted Brown's martyrdom.

From New York City, Horace Greeley pursued the same theme as Thurlow Weed. On October 21, a few days after Brown's capture, an editorial in the *Tribune* insisted that he had been a peaceful man until he moved to Kansas, where slaveholders committed outrages against him and his family. Then, after dismissing the claims that abolitionists and Republicans were involved with Brown, the newspaper attributed the incident to the evils of slavery. A month later, and with Brown's execution date drawing near, the *Tribune* warned that slaveholders in Virginia were accomplishing Brown's purpose "by their invention of an abolitionist conspiracy and warnings of slave uprisings."[21] Such warnings would serve only to agitate the slave population.

As was the case with several of the major northern newspapers, the *Tribune* sent a correspondent to Richmond, Virginia, where Brown was being held. Throughout November 1859 the newspaper published almost daily reports from its correspondent. He not only conveyed Brown's spoken and written words, in which the prisoner portrayed himself as having no regrets about what he had done, quoted scripture at length, and welcomed his upcoming martyrdom, but also commented on Virginians' fear of an abolitionist attack to free the convicted man and on the overall sense of fear and hatred Virginians evidenced toward northerners. In addition the reporter noted growing sentiment in favor of secession.[22]

Rather than seeing the raid as a reason for Virginians to consider secession, the Harrisburg, Pennsylvania, *Telegraph* urged southerners to recognize that northerners would not countenance attacks on southerners and would join with them in subduing slave insurrections. The newspaper insisted that the fact that the federal government had dispatched troops to Virginia after the incident was proof that the government was the protector of the South and not its enemy. The *Telegraph* declared that "the union is essential to the well being of the South as well as the North."[23]

In the West, the Republican Chicago *Tribune,* after describing Brown as crazy, laid blame for his madness at the door of slaveholders in Kansas. Never missing an opportunity to attack Stephen A. Douglas, the *Tribune* declared the Kansas problem to be the result of Douglas's undoing of the Missouri Compromise. In an October 21 editorial, it labeled Brown as no worse than Jefferson Davis, because "each would destroy the Union." It was up to Republicans to save it. After Brown's conviction, the *Tribune* addressed the question of whether, as so many southern newspapers claimed, he was guilty of treason. The distinction was one between a war against slavery and a war against the Union. For the Chicago *Tribune,* only the latter constituted treason.[24] The *Tribune* insisted that Brown believed that slavery, not the Union, was his enemy, and thus he was innocent of treason.

In its coverage of the attack and its aftermath, while employing the same arguments as other Republican newspapers, the Indianapolis *Journal* put particular stress on the theme that what threatened the well-being of white southerners was not the efforts of a handful of abolitionist conspirators but rather the institution of slavery, which by its nature always carried the threat of insurrection on the part of those it enslaved. Thus, the newspaper argued, it was slaveholders and not abolitionists who were the threat to the South and the nation. According to the *Journal,* slavery carried the seeds of societal destruction, and slaveholders wanted to spread slavery to all the Republic.[25] Slavery was and would continue to be, the Milwaukee *Daily Free Democrat* asserted, accompanied by "servile insurrections" that would "stop only when slavery [was] ended."[26]

Dialogues in both regions were altered significantly as a result of the action of twenty-two armed men. Those dialogues concerned the role of slavery in America, the character of northerners and the character of southerners, the respect for law, and the use of violence on the part of people in both regions. Some southern newspapers used what happened at Harpers Ferry as proof that northerners condoned, even engaged in, acts of treason against the Republic and threatened the safety of southern people. To those newspapers, only secession from the Union would preserve, at least in the South, the heritage of the Founders, the principles that defined the Republic. Those newspapers also saw the attack as a warning about what might happen if northern "fanatics" gained control of the federal government. More than ever before, the newspapers described Republicans not as an opposing political party but as abolitionist fanatics. As expressed in most of the southern press, comfort in the belief that most northerners were devoted to the protection of the rights— constitutionally guaranteed—of white southerners to hold slaves as property was shaken if not entirely destroyed. Would those northerners risk the Union for the sake of ending slavery, and would they condone some of their brethren's use of illegal and barbaric means to accomplish that goal? Southern newspapers told readers that it seemed likely the answer was yes. Those newspapers were moving closer to conveying a common message about the character of northerners, their evil intent, and the tactics they would employ to carry out a plot against the South and the Republic. Should a northern political party, the Republican Party, attain power, the inference was that the South would consider the party illegitimate and refuse to be governed by it.

In the North, questions of the raid's purpose, and who was responsible for it, were answered in terms of predictable political partisanship. But prominent in the rhetoric that newspapers on both political sides employed was the suggestion of the danger of disunion, the undermining of republican society, and the abandonment of the heritage of the Founding Fathers. Each side accused the other of putting politics above national interest.

Writing the day after Brown and his cohort were convicted and sentenced to die, Milwaukee editor Sherman Booth angrily attacked the trial and the verdict and saw in it the evil of southern power and southern ways. In the South, Booth told readers, "The man who writes an abolition sentiment is strung to the highest tree—the press that pretends to freedom of opinion is thrown into the nearest river."[27] Having condemned southern intolerance of opinions with which they disagreed and having labeled Virginians, in whose state Brown was tried, convicted, and would be hanged, as barbarians in whose hands republican principles would be crushed, the editor went on to assure readers that "violence is associated with slavery and slave holders not with Republicans." What should be done to Democrats in Wisconsin, he contin- ued, was to "hang them—hang them higher than Haman on a gibbet of pub- lic opinion, and nail them there as an example to all traitors to our laws and institutions."

When a Republican was elected president just over a year after John Brown and his compatriots attacked the arsenal in Harpers Ferry, the power of the debate over slavery to divide society, and the ability of the Republic to survive that division, was to be tested. For many northerners, and many southerners as well, John Brown had set the match to the powder keg. Could it be extin- guished before the powder exploded? The press posed the American dilemma in the months before and immediately after the election of 1860.

6   Lincoln's Election:
Could a Republican Lead the Republic?

On May 16, 1860, six months after John Brown's execution, the Republicans convened in Chicago. The pre-convention favorite and leader in the delegate count on the first two ballots, William Seward of New York, was unable to gain the support necessary to be the party's nominee for the presidency. Delegates then turned to Abraham Lincoln of Illinois. The impact of the Harpers Ferry incident was still a raw wound in the North. Seward was closely identified with abolitionists. Lincoln was not. Seward's views were well known. Lincoln's views, despite the national attention paid to his debates with Stephen Douglas in the 1858 campaign for Douglas's Illinois seat in the U.S. Senate, were relatively unknown. Lincoln's allies portrayed him as a moderate on the slavery issue, whereas Seward was labeled a radical. As Republican Party leaders read the situation, thanks in large measure to John Brown, a moderate and not a radical was the party's best hope to win the presidency. Both their reading of northern public opinion after Brown's execution and congressional actions in the late winter and early spring of 1860 had set the stage for the Republican convention.

When Congress convened in the early weeks of 1860, evidence of the polarizing effect of Harpers Ferry soon became apparent. In February, Sen. Jefferson Davis of Mississippi offered a series of resolutions that were backed by southerners either committed to or, like Davis, inclined to secession of their states from the Union. Davis proposed a bill that would protect a slaveholder's right to own slaves in any territory. He proposed a resolution asserting that no state had a right to interfere with the institutions of another state. And he called upon Congress to declare that any attack on slavery constituted a violation of the federal Constitution. In late May, soon after the Republicans had selected Lincoln to lead their ticket in the fall, Davis and his allies prevailed on the Senate to pass his resolutions. The affirmative vote angered northern Democrats. By that time the Party of Jackson was in disarray.

The Democrats convened in Charleston, South Carolina, in late April. Stephen A. Douglas was the choice of northern Democrats, but the strong southern wing of the party rejected the Illinois senator who had opposed and ultimately defeated the Lecompton Constitution. The delegates endured fifty-seven ballots without determining a nominee. They reassembled in Baltimore some six weeks later. When many delegates from the Lower South walked out of that assembly, Douglas's supporters secured the nomination for him. Ten days later southern dissidents held their own convention in Baltimore and chose John C. Breckinridge of Kentucky as their candidate.

Abraham Lincoln's opponents, by fighting among themselves and by dividing, had assured his election in the fall. From May to December 1860, newspapers devoted a great deal of space to describing the Illinois lawyer and presenting what they perceived to be his views on the issues that troubled so many Americans that summer and fall. The character depicted in those newspapers' descriptions and the explanations of his views varied wildly, depending on the politics and the regional location of each publication. Readers of Republican newspapers read descriptions of a man who valued the Union above all else and believed southerners were entitled to hold slaves in their own states. Nevertheless, he would stand firm against southern bullying of northerners for the sake of expanding slavery beyond its then-current boundaries. Lincoln, those readers were told, would defend the character of northerners against the seemingly never-ending assaults of southerners and make clear northerners' loyalty to the Republic and all for which it stood.[1]

For well over a century historians have studied the texts of Abraham Lincoln's speeches and letters, seeking to determine just where he stood on the key issues of his time. For all of that study, however, definitive answers are illusive. Was Lincoln unsure of where he stood? Did his positions change as events unfolded? Did political circumstances dictate a strategy of avoiding rather than asserting clear answers to complex questions? Probably all of those questions should be answered in the affirmative.

But if historians find in Lincoln's speeches and letters both complexity and ambiguity, newspaper editors of both regions and all parties provided descriptions of the man that, whatever else, were clear and direct. The newspapers brooked no subtlety from a would-be political leader. As newspapers shaped their readers' sense of the reality of events, so, too, did they describe public figures. Who Abraham Lincoln was and what he represented could be gleaned from daily newspaper descriptions, and, depending on the region and the politics of the newspaper, that sense of the man varied dramatically. There was Lincoln the Black Republican abolitionist. There was Lincoln the ignorant and unsophisticated tool of evil politicians. There was Lincoln the simple, honest, and direct but reasonable representative of the average American, a man in politics but not of it, and more. Because Americans knew so little about the man, it was left to the press to bring him to life. Republicans may have chosen Lincoln as their nominee because they perceived him to be a moderate who had separated himself from abolitionists, but readers of most southern newspapers were told that as a Black Republican the Illinoisan was their enemy. Most, although not all, southern newspapers insisted that secession would be the appropriate response should Lincoln be elected.

Notwithstanding these threats of secession, in the fall of 1860, when a majority of northern men went to the polls to cast their ballots for Abraham Lincoln, did they do so with any reasonable expectation that a Republican victory would result in the division of the Union followed by war? Based on the content of Republican newspapers, the answer was no. Southerners had threatened secession before without carrying out the threat. Indeed, any concession by the Republican press that postelection events would unfold as they did might have resulted in a different election outcome.

Although the northern Democratic press as well as all the southern press had warned of the consequences of a Lincoln election, the Republican press's answer was to dismiss the dire forecasts of the consequences of a Lincoln victory either as more typical southern whining or as a Democratic Party tactic to scare voters away from the Republican candidate. The Republican press assured readers that southern unionists would not allow the fire-eater extremists to control events. Southerners, they argued, knew that the Republican Party would neither interfere with slavery where it existed nor tolerate any efforts to deny southerners their rights, including and especially their right to their slave property.

Republican newspapers dismissed claims made by both the northern and southern Democratic press that the Republican Party sought to foment a slave insurrection. Those editors were convinced, and sought to convince readers, that the roots of the Republic were too deep in southern soil to be torn out by those who called for rebellion. The darkest thought that Republican editors expressed was that radical-extremist South Carolinians might take their state out of the Union, and perhaps Mississippi would do the same, but no other southern state would follow. Republican newspapers held that those prodigal children, isolated and too weak economically to survive on their own, would in time return to the fold. Lincoln himself believed that southern unionists were in a majority in their region and would prevail.

Both Republicans and some northern Democrats misunderstood southern public opinion. They had failed to realize or acknowledge that a number of events had made southerners deeply and fundamentally distrustful of what they labeled the "Black Republican abolitionists." So, too, did southern unionists miscalculate. They were convinced that the majority of northerners, the "conservative majority," would reject a Republican candidate for president. They thought that northerners would put the Union ahead of abolition and vote Democratic. Even in the last month before the election, with a Lincoln victory a real possibility, southern unionists held to the hope that the northern conservative majority would force Lincoln to negotiate with the South and so assure the credibility of southern unionist claims that the North meant the South no harm.

Two days after Abraham Lincoln was elected, the Washington, D.C., *National Intelligencer,* which had urged voters to save the Union by voting for John Bell, pleaded with readers to recognize that the Republican's election would "neither change the Constitution nor the laws of the land."[2] The newspaper recalled the fears in 1800, when Jefferson was elected, that the Republic would be destroyed and anarchy would reign. Noting the internal dissension and secessionist feelings that threatened the unity of neighboring Mexico, the editor insisted that "as Anglo-Saxons, Americans should show they are superior and make self-government work."[3]

In the months between the election and inauguration of Lincoln, notwithstanding the secession of South Carolina and several other southern states, the *Intelligencer* continued to plead with the South to give Lincoln a chance. Two days after the inauguration, it pointed out that the new president had pledged in his inauguration speech that he did "not intend to interfere with slavery where it is" and would "respect the Constitution." Moreover, the editor lectured readers on the point that Lincoln asked "for a candid hearing and a fair trial—all citizens should give him this."[4]

Some three weeks later, with the conflict of ideas and emotions clearly verging on a conflict of arms, the *Intelligencer* despaired of any hope that reason and truth would prevail. The newspaper's gloomy words on the character of public debate were evidently aimed at politicians but were certainly stated broadly enough to include the newspapers that amplified politicians' words and, through reiteration and emphasis, made heated words even hotter. The *Intelligencer*'s sad assessment of political rhetoric and its effect is worth quoting at some length. Consider these words published on March 30, 1861, when war seemed to many to be unavoidable and less than two weeks before Fort Sumter was shelled. Seven states had seceded by March 30: South Carolina, Mississippi, Florida, Alabama, Georgia, Louisiana, and Texas. Also by that date a provisional government called the Confederate States of America had been formed, and Jefferson Davis had been inaugurated as its president. Small wonder that the *Intelligencer* declared:

> Not the least among the anomalous characteristics of the evil day upon which we have fallen is the spirit of rancor and intolerance with which honest differences of opinion are treated by political opponents. Gratuitous malevolence, combining with public discord seems, in some cases, to have taxed its ingenuity in order to asperse and blacken the reputations of those whose only crime has been, at the most, an error in judgement. The vocabulary of abuse has been exhausted in order to furnish invective for the gratification of partisan spite and animosity, insomuch that the current disrespect for the obligations of truth has been only equaled by an impudent contempt for the rules of common decency.

Given the language politicians and newspapers used, what the *Intelligencer* meant by "the vocabulary of abuse" and the "contempt for the rules of common decency" was clear. Had the press used different, more measured, vocabulary and shown respect for the rules of common decency would the political process that had held the Republic together up to that time have continued to work, and would the division of the Union, followed by war, have been avoided? Did the press have such power over readers? We can only guess at an answer.

The prospect of the election—and then the actual election—of Abraham Lincoln was unwelcome but tolerated by a few border South and Democratic North newspapers that took a position similar to that of the Washington *Intelligencer*. But more commonly in the South, angry and devoid of any hope that what they perceived to be southern rights and security would be protected by Black Republicans, newspapers moved to a secessionist position. In the case of northern newspapers, Democratic editors called on Lincoln to resist the pressures within his party's abolitionist wing and follow the course that a traditional Whig would take—stressing economic progress while repressing the slavery issue. By so doing, they argued, the South would be placated, and its states would remain in the Union. Some Republican newspapers offered similar advice, although the majority urged Lincoln to demonstrate "back-bone" and "manliness" and call the South's bluff. Those editors told the Republican president not to spoil southerners as Democratic presidents had done. The South could no longer be allowed to rant and rave and cry secession if it did not get what it wanted.

These were the positions. While considering the press's arguments and the rhetoric in which they were couched, we must keep in mind the *Intelligencer*'s admonitions regarding the vocabulary used and how those words could have contributed to distrust on both sides.

Abraham Lincoln was at the center of this maelstrom. His only federal political experience up to 1860 had been as a one-term Whig Party member elected to the House of Representatives from Illinois, his home for most of his adult life. He had lost his congressional seat in 1849, primarily because of his opposition to the Mexican War. Following that defeat he resumed his law career. If Lincoln conjured up any image of himself it was that of the poor boy who made good. It was certainly not that of a crusading reformer bent on the destruction of slavery. In 1858 the Illinois lawyer reappeared as a candidate for public office, campaigning for a seat in the U.S. Senate against his long-time acquaintance and fellow Springfield lawyer Stephen Douglas. From his position as senator from Illinois, Douglas had carved out a prominent place in national politics. When he agreed to tour the state and debate with Lincoln the goal of both candidates was to influence state legislative election races, because state legislators chose U.S. senators. Douglas retained enough support to keep his Senate seat, but Lincoln's name, thanks to newspaper coverage of the debates, became known beyond his city and state.

Lincoln's position on slavery could be summarized as belief that slavery was wrong, that it should not be allowed to expand beyond its current borders, and that eventually, and by orderly and legal means, it should expire. Until that happened, however, slaveholders should be accorded their right of property and be made to feel secure from the threat of servile insurrection. As for the slaves, Lincoln described them as being of a race clearly inferior to whites but entitled to the fruits of their labor.[5] In that sense, but only in that sense, were they like all other Americans. Those were positions with which both the free-soil and old Whig wings of the Republican Party could live.

Had the newspapers sought to find out about the Republican presidential candidate's position regarding slavery, that is what they would have reported to readers. But things had reached a point where, as the *National Intelligencer* described it, evidence was not what most newspapers sought. Passion had conquered logic and reason. Lincoln's assurances, both before the election and in his inaugural address, that the South was in no danger from his administration did not ring true to most southern and northern Democratic editors and probably to most of their readers. The fact was that a Black Republican had been elected president. Although it was true that the Democrats had a majority in both houses of Congress, doubts now existed that northern Democrats, such as Douglas, could be counted upon to remain loyal to the party and receptive to the concerns and wishes of the South. Even if that majority did provide some security, how long would it be before Republicans won control of the legislative bodies?

Lincoln may have claimed he was no abolitionist, but to many southerners it was a case of guilt by association. For them, Lincoln was a covert abolitionist if not an overt one. To growing numbers of southerners, the Black Republicans were an illegitimate political party, and southerners saw no obligation to accept its right to assume governmental control. Thus they had every right and reason to separate themselves from a government controlled by such a party. As southern newspapers described it, a republic led by Black Republicans was no republic in which decent and freedom-loving people could live.

American political tradition dictated that presidential candidates wait at their homes during a campaign so voters could call them to office or not. But in October 1860, a month before the election, Stephen Douglas left Springfield, Illinois, on a campaign tour of the South. It may have been a desperate attempt to win support for his candidacy in that region, or it may have been an attempt to persuade southerners that they should accept the result and remain in the Union if Lincoln won.[6] In his speeches on that southern tour Douglas often made that plea for the Union. Sparks of unionist sentiment remained aglow in the South, especially in commercial centers where the prospect of disunion raised fears of business collapse.

On October 25 Douglas arrived in Memphis, a major cotton buying and shipping center on the Mississippi River. The Memphis *Appeal,* already announced as supporting Douglas, declared the Illinois senator to be "the great tribune of the American people" and the "enemy of the fire-eater and the abolitionist." In an editorial on October 26, a day after describing the enthusiastic crowd that greeted Douglas, the newspaper insisted that fire-eaters wanted Lincoln to win the election because it would give them the weapon they needed to convince southerners to secede from the Union. After the Lincoln victory, the *Appeal* honored Douglas's plea for acceptance of the results of a legitimate election and noted his fear for the future of the Republic. The newspaper posed a rhetorical question: "Shall we remain under the jurisdiction of the Federal government and demand our constitutional rights in the Union or shall we desert it and violate our faith?"[7] The faith to which the *Appeal* referred was the heritage of the Founding Fathers, the Republic. The editor concluded that southerners should stay in the Union "until or unless the Constitution is violated." He urged readers to give the Lincoln administration a chance to show how it would treat the South.

In New Orleans, the *Bee,* which had supported the Tennessean John Bell and the Constitutional Union Party, struck the same note as the *Appeal.* In an

October 18 editorial it acknowledged that Lincoln was likely to win. "Are we, therefore," the *Bee* asked, "to give up every thing; to consider the South ruined and disgraced and be ready, with desperate and bloody hands, to pull down upon our heads the beautiful and massive fabric of the Union?" The editor reminded readers that Democrats would still control Congress, that a majority of northerners were devoted to preserving the Union, and that the antislavery party would be impotent. A few days later the *Bee* renewed its attack on secessionists and insisted that whatever the South's grievances they did not warrant leaving the Union. It also characterized secessionists as "the chivalry, all words and high flown rhetoric but impractical men." Such men, the editor assured, were centuries out of date.[8]

When Lincoln was elected, the *Bee* pronounced him chosen "legally and constitutionally" and urged readers to wait and watch, "to stand by the Union as long as it respects our rights."[9] But by December 20, 1861, the eve of South Carolina's vote to secede, the newspaper had significantly changed its position. The editor asked, "If other cotton states secede how can Louisiana desert them?" As for the conservative northern majority to whom the editor had looked hopefully a month earlier, he now believed that "all the prayers and entreaties of the Northern minority [the conservatives] will prove as ineffective towards prolonging the duration of the Union as have the mingled menaces and derision of the abolition majority of that section."[10] The editorial concluded with the assertion that the South was acting in self-defense and that it "can get independence, respect and safety outside the Union." On Christmas Day 1860, the *Bee* informed readers that "any idea that Black Republicans will make the necessary concessions to the South are gone. Secession is the only answer."

A week before the president-elect was to be inaugurated, the *Bee* offered an assessment of the man. Lincoln, it said, lacked the intellectual skill, the strength, and the competence to resist the "ultra Black Republican faction." Writing the next day, the editor noted that "the States which have withdrawn did so deliberately and dispassionately, because they are firmly convinced of the impossibility of preserving their rights, their interests, or their honor under a perverted and violated constitution."[11]

A number of southern newspapers that supported either Douglas or Bell took the stance of the *Appeal* and the initial position of the *Bee*, pleading for the South to stay in the Union even if Lincoln were elected. But events occurred with dizzying swiftness and had a kaleidoscopic effect. The months between election day and inauguration saw southern states parading out of the Union, the formation of the Confederacy, and the inauguration on February 23, 1861, of Jefferson Davis as president of that Confederacy. In that crisis, many unionist newspapers joined ranks with those supporting secession.

For every southern newspaper that called for calm and patience if Lincoln were elected and continued that call immediately after his election there were many more that saw the prospect of a Black Republican in the seat of power as a threat to southern "interests, rights and honor." The Nashville *Whig* had warned that the crisis the country faced "was not of slavery but was a crisis because of those who would use it to build a party."[12] In short politics, not principle, was at the heart of the national dilemma. But as is so often the case, one person's principle was another person's politics.

In the wake of Lincoln's election, the Richmond *Enquirer* declared the government to now be in the hands of the enemies of slavery.[13] The Augusta *Constitutionalist* told readers after the election that the South saw "'the flag as soon to pass to abolitionists bent on destroying slavery.'"[14] Three weeks after the election, the Richmond *Enquirer* assured readers that "this is not the Government which the Constitution authorizes" and insisted that "there will be, in reality, no Constitution or fundamental law."[15] The Gallatin, Tennessee, *Examiner,* following the same line, declared that "'the gloom which now hangs over the Union is the result of Northern fanaticism. The South has ever been loyal to the Union.'"[16] In Charleston, South Carolina, the *Courier,* which to this point had been the more moderate of that city's newspapers, issued a dire forecast if Lincoln were elected: "'If in our present position of power and unitedness we have the raid of John Brown, and twenty towns burned down in Texas in one year by abolitionists [a widely circulated but false rumor], what will be the measures of insurrection and incendiarism which must follow our notorious and abject prostration to abolition rule in Washington, with all of the patronage of the Federal government and a Union organization in the South to support it? Secret conspiracy and its attended horrors, with rumors of more horrors, will hover over every portion of the South.'"[17]

The *Courier* also noted that although property (slaves) would be lost, far more could follow: liberty, home, country, and everything that makes life worth having. "'And this loss will probably take place under circumstances of suffering and horror unparalleled in the history of nations. We must preserve our liberties and institutions under penalties greater than those which impend over any people in the world.'"[18] It must have been easy for readers to think a possible civil war a small price to pay in contrast to that which otherwise they would be subjected. While defending their property and lives they also would be defending the liberty for which the Republic had been created.

Two days after it received word of Lincoln's election on November 6, 1860, the *Courier* pronounced "the beginning of the revolution" and pleaded for "resolute, deliberate, cool and determined action." It was adamant that "the enemy. . . . stares us in the face and we must either make him surrender or he will complete our destruction. There is no loophole from which to escape."[19]

With varying degrees of enthusiasm, sooner or later the great majority of southern newspapers came to the conclusion that secession and—if the federal government sought to prevent secession—war were the only courses of action southerners could take. As those newspapers described it, however devoted they were, the Union was now either entirely, or soon to be entirely, in control of abolitionists. And abolitionists, of course, were fanatics who would ignore the dictates of the Constitution, violate the laws of the land, behave in barbaric fashion, and condone such behavior for the sake of carrying out their agenda. Newspapers insisted that the northern agenda included the denial of southern rights of property in the form of slaves and destruction of southern economic interests in general.

Beyond property rights and economic interest, southern editors raised the specter of threats to the physical safety of southern men, women, and children. Those editors proclaimed that risks were taken for the sake of affirming the equality of an inferior race, thus trampling on southern honor by dismissing concerns about rights and safety as mere whining on the part of a selfish and treacherous people. In the face of the perceived reality of men who had those intentions controlling the government, southern newspapers saw their region as withdrawing from the Union because it had forfeited its right to command loyalty. As described in almost all southern newspapers, it was northerners who subverted the heritage of the Founders and were sacrificing the Republic. If the Republic were to survive as the Founders created it, society had to keep fanatics at bay. When they chose the title "Confederate States" for their new nation, a reference to its first constitution, the Articles of Confederation, secessionists were sending a clear message about their loyalty to the Republic.

In the North, editorial polarities were reversed. Perhaps what is most striking but unsurprising about the northern newspapers' view of things was that editors of a number of Democratic publications expressed at least some degree of sympathy with the South. In the months following Lincoln's election, southern political party lines tended to fade, and sectional interests tended to strengthen to the point where party identity blurred and all but disappeared. In the North, the election of a Republican president, at least initially, seemed to harden party identities and positions. Each side was preoccupied with blaming the crisis on leaders of, and strategies employed by, the other. Even after the firing on Fort Sumter, the northern press stood divided over who to blame for the crisis and how the Union should respond (chapter 7). Party allegiance determined the lines of that division.

On election day, November 6, 1860, the New York *Herald* wrote about what it believed and feared would be the consequences of a Lincoln victory. Lincoln, it insisted, was committed to ending slavery, and the South was committed to resisting that effort, even if it meant splintering the Union. The editor declared that southerners "must resist because their society, their law and order depends on slavery. The crisis is union or disunion." Two days later, on November 8, and with the election results clear, the *Herald* lectured the president-elect about what he must do to avoid the impending disaster. He must choose between harmonizing his party or his country. The call for party unity referred to the split in the Republican Party between former free-soilers and abolitionists on the one hand and former northern Whigs and Democrats on the other. The president-elect was urged to enforce the Fugitive Slave Law and to "silence the abolitionists in his party."

The *Herald* warned that South Carolina would secede and that the Republican president, once in office, should invite the state to rejoin the Union and certainly not coerce it. On November 9 the newspaper urged Lincoln and his supporters to assure the South that they would not interfere with slavery and reminded readers that secession would hurt New York's commerce and greatly diminish America's economic and political position in the world. James Gordon Bennett led associates at the *Herald* in consistently emphasizing the importance of practical, rather than ideological, concerns determining the course of action. The following week the newspaper chastised "religious fanatics and a fanatical press" for causing all the trouble.[20]

Throughout the winter the *Herald* recorded with dismay the southern desertion of the Union, state by state, and criticized Lincoln, who had yet to take office, for his failure to act to keep seceding states in the Union. Having earlier told Lincoln in an editorial not to placate the abolitionists in his party, Bennett accused the president-elect of having done just that and seeking to "please the altruists of the northeast and northwest."[21] According to the *Herald,* Lincoln had played politics instead of harmonizing the country. With eight states gone from the Union, Bennett instructed the president-elect to compromise in any and every way possible to keep the remaining seven slave states from seceding. One way to do that was to avoid conflict with seceded states over forts and revenue. The newspaper predicted, however, that the incoming administration would not follow such advice.

On inauguration day, March 4, 1861, Bennett laid blame for the national crisis on Lincoln's election and on the fact that the Republican Party was a minority party "whose principles are alien to a majority of the people." The *Herald* also identified Lincoln with the radical wing of his party, which it likened to "the Jacobeans of the French Revolution." The following day the *Herald* analyzed the president's inaugural address, describing it as full of "vague generalities" and lacking any sense of urgency, all seen as evidence of Lincoln's "craft and cunning" if nothing else. On March 6, the newspaper reiterated that Lincoln was a minority president who had "no place in the affections of the people at large." As each day passed, the *Herald* offered what it believed to be proof that the Republican president was controlled by abolitionists, and those fanatics wanted war.

Northern Democratic newspapers expressed many of the same opinions and concerns. The Cincinnati *Enquirer,* which warned of calamity to the country if the "Republican-abolitionist" won, was only one of a number of publications that described Republicans and abolitionists as one and the same.[22] In an odd twist a week after the election, and having declared disaster if Lincoln did win, the *Enquirer* speculated that it expected that "disunion in the South [would] recede partly because Abolitionists want them to leave the Union."[23]

In Philadelphia, John Forney's *Press,* while supporting Douglas in the election, conceded in an October 23 editorial that Lincoln would win Pennsylvania and the election. The editor called on readers to denounce disunionists even though it meant splitting the Democratic Party and urged Lincoln to court the pro-Union people in the South. The *Press* advised the Republican to proclaim himself "the friend and protector of all their [the South's] rights under the Constitution."

A few days later, the *Press* wondered whether a Lincoln administration could be any worse for the South than the Buchanan administration had been for the North. The implication was that the North had not left the Union despite being governed by a president who many considered to be hostile to their interests, so why should the South take such an extreme step? The editor followed by declaring, "We have the best system of government the world has ever known. We can't destroy it. It is the duty of every man, wherever he lives, to support the government and avoid anarchy."[24] With the election results in hand and sounding like those few southern newspapers that supported Douglas, the *Press* declared Lincoln's victory "a verdict for perpetual union" and went on to remind readers that the Republican was "constitutionally chosen." Then, urging readers to "give him a chance," the *Press* noted the president-elect was pledged to carry out the provisions of the Fugitive Slave Act.[25]

In the days that followed the election, Forney attacked southern extremists, whom he described as a "large class of people. . . . who look to disunion for their own ambitions and pecuniary purposes." The editor also despaired at the "torrent of fanaticism in the South" and called on men in the North of both parties "to unite on behalf of the Union."[26] This was a rare instance of a northern Democratic newspaper urging the parties to set aside their differences for the sake of sectional unity. A unified North should then assure the South of protection against servile insurrection and be devoted to the preservation of the Constitution and the Union. Forney labeled secession as treason.

In the weeks that followed, the *Press* denounced the conspiracies it detected against the Union and the loss of the spirit of patriotism and declared that there were "traitors in our midst."[27] On January 5, having identified all that danger to the Union, the newspaper speculated optimistically that "when the Southern people are convinced that their fellow-countrymen in the free States intend no attack upon them but desire only to see the Constitution obeyed and the laws made under it enforced, they will probably consent to listen to such terms of peace and reconciliation as have been, and no doubt will be, offered to them." What might be termed a gentle but firm approach to misbehaving children rarely was evident in the Democratic press, but it was the rule in Republican newspapers.

Assuming that southern newspapers reflected the views of their readers, southerners believed that the election of Abraham Lincoln was a clear statement that abolitionists were now in charge of the federal government and that as a consequence both the South and the Republic would be destroyed in the name of their fanatical cause. But Republican newspapers hammered home the argument that a Lincoln victory would end the national crisis and not exacerbate it. As a preelection theme it obviously was a good tactic for gaining support for their candidate, but the postelection statement of the point suggests that in fact those Republicans believed that Lincoln could ameliorate sectional tensions.

After all, as the Republican press saw it, Lincoln had made clear that he was no abolitionist and no fanatic. He was born a southerner, he understood the South and the role slavery played in the region, and he acknowledged the superiority of the white race. He had pledged to support the Constitution and carry out the laws of the land. Surely the majority, if not the fire-eater minority in the South, would be comforted that they and their institutions would be safe when Lincoln assumed the presidency. And the Republican press found yet another reason for assuming that, with the Republican victory, the Republic would be saved.

Republican editors predicted that Lincoln would stand firm where his Democratic predecessor had been weak. Buchanan had supported the Lecompton Constitution even though it thwarted the will of the majority in Kansas. Buchanan had even proposed in his final State of the Union address in January

1861, when he was a lame duck, that the Constitution be amended to allow slavery everywhere in the Union. Lincoln, however, would not bow to the pressure of the slave-power oligarchy. He would make clear to those obstreperous children what the rules were. They, faced with a sympathetic but determined father, would then stop pushing the North and trying its patience.

Many Republican editors believed that the firm but fair approach would turn disorder into harmony. It did not take long, however, before those editors were convinced that the wayward children would not behave and that southerners saw Lincoln as vindictive and determined to punish them for what, as a fanatic abolitionist, he saw as the sin of slavery. Most southern newspapers insisted that Black Republican rule could not be thought of as anything but malevolent as it concerned southerners. There was no choice but to break up the family. Northern newspapers of whatever party or affiliation were left troubled and unsure how to react as, one by one but in quick order, the "cotton states" followed South Carolina out of the Union. Most newspapers shifted their stance on the questions of why and whose fault it was that the Union was being divided, whether secession was good or bad for the Republic, and whether southern states should be allowed to walk away peacefully or coerced into remaining in the Union.

On November 7, 1860, the Republican Harrisburg, Pennsylvania, *Telegraph,* with the election decided in favor of its candidate, headlined its editorial page with the words "THE UNION SAVED!" and followed, still in boldface type, with "Treason Crushed Out—The Fusionists Confused" (a reference to northern Democrats). The next day, the editor assured readers that Lincoln's "election settles all the issues that have entered into the contest, slavery extension, secession, and what just now is probably still more vital, the equal right of the free with the slave States to share in the administration of the Federal Government." Moreover, "we shall probably hear no more . . . of the cry of secession or disunion." The piece concluded with the assurance that people, now that the will of the majority had been established, could get back to being "the most prosperous and the happiest people on earth." In short, the Republic had been saved.

Some other Republican newspapers shared that misplaced optimism. The Chicago *Tribune* editorialized on November 9 that although the Republican Party was now a force only in the North it soon would be accepted everywhere and, the editor assured readers, the party had a national agenda. The *Tribune* acknowledged the threats of secession emanating from the South but considered them serious only in South Carolina and Mississippi and wrote off both states as being so small in population as not to matter.

On election day the New York *Tribune* assured readers near and far that "once the South realizes that Republicans are not going to end slavery in the

States that things will settle down and the slaveholders will soon learn to submit with a good grace to a transfer of political power." In contrast to descriptions of the Republican Party as a band of radical fanatics, in reality it "attracted the solid, sober, intelligent middle class." The account concluded by offering a slogan: "All together now for Justice, Peace and Freedom."[28] Two days later the *Tribune,* on news of more secessionist talk in South Carolina, urged people there to consider carefully what they were doing and concluded that if they wanted to leave the Union they should be allowed to do so.[29]

Even in the face of secessionist talk in South Carolina, optimism about the future of the Union characterized the immediate postelection reaction of the Indianapolis *Journal,* whose editor dismissed talk of disunion. "It will never amount to more than words, and if it does it can only damage those who are engaged in it. The Union is too strong and too good, to suffer from the madness of such men."[30] In slave-state Missouri, the now-Republican St. Louis *Missouri Democrat* assured readers that disunionists were a minority in a minority of states, that a Lincoln election will not mean a revolt, and that the southern majority would "put down the traitors in their midst."[31] The editor concluded with the assurance that "secessionists are few and weak." On November 7, with Lincoln a winner, the newspaper headlined "Victory and Peace" but acknowledged that to assure the latter the "enemies of the Union" had to be "compelled to submit to the laws. Treason must be extinguished." Then the editor reminded readers that Lincoln was pledged not to interfere with slavery where it already existed. It was treason against the Republic, not slavery in America, that had to be extinguished.

On December 20, 1860, on what turned out to be the eve of South Carolina's formal departure from the Union, the Harrisburg *Telegraph* addressed what it thought the act of secession would mean for the Republic. The editor began by noting that it was frequently said that secession is a revolution. "It is revolution," he argued, "but in a far wider sense than is generally understood." Secession could lead to only one end: anarchy. As applied to the South it would mean the imposition of "the aristocratic idea, and that the ideals of the republic will be destroyed." "The grand principle of the Declaration of Independence [presumably that all men are created equal] would be repudiated." Furthermore, the real victims of secession would be white southern workers.

On December 22, with South Carolina secession now a reality, the *Telegraph*'s editorial page carried the headline "Disunion and Treason." The newspaper warned that the "destruction of the Republic" had never been so imminent and that people did not realize what was happening. It also bemoaned the fact that the federal government, still in Democratic Party hands, was too corrupt, weak, and lacking in moral courage to respond. The *Telegraph* con-cluded that the only hope was for "a prompt uprising of the patriotic people, who do not love CAESAR less but Rome more. It must be done and done quick-ly, for in a short time the grandest Government the world ever saw may be utterly ruined, and the genius of liberty, with saddened heart, will weep over the irreparable wrong to freedom and human progress." The editor did not reveal just how patriotic people should act, but he did make it clear that more compromises to placate the South were not the answer.

Obviously, the secession from the Union of the cotton states by the end of January 1861, and the formal organization soon thereafter of those states into the Confederate States of America, changed the outlook of the Republi-can press. As optimism gave way to pessimism, attention shifted from the question of whether southerners would actually abandon the Republic and rebel against the heritage of the Founding Fathers to questions of how to treat the rebels and who was responsible for their unruly behavior.

In mid-November 1860, the New York *Tribune* sent a correspondent to Charleston to report on discussions that had been underway even before Lin-coln's election and would conclude with the Palmetto State's declaration of independence from the Union. By late November, based on the reports tele-graphed back to New York, the newspaper told readers to assume that South Carolinians, controlled by a small cohort of "traitors," would secede.[32]

Speculating on what would follow, Horace Greeley's newspaper argued that other states, although they did not want to secede, would use the threat of it to win concessions from the federal government. The danger of that strat-egy was that if their bluff were called and no concessions made they would have to secede as a matter of honor. The *Tribune* continued to insist that no force should be used to keep states from leaving the Union, but it now began to raise such issues as payment of some sort to the federal government for the cost of acquiring the territory of any seceding state.[33] Readers must have won-dered a bit about the logic and certainly the practicality of that argument, which represented a shift from the position of letting them go in peace and without conditions. The *Tribune* now would insist on conditions.

In the wake of South Carolina's formal departure from the Union, the *Tri-bune* declared its people to have engaged in an act of "rebellion and treason." Treason does not go unpunished. In a January 10, 1861, editorial, after report-ing that Mississippi had seceded, the newspaper asked rhetorical questions: "Shall our Federal Union be extinguished by rebellion?—our Constitution de-stroyed by treachery and force?—the City of Washington seized and plundered by a lawless mob?—the Federal Congress dispersed, never again to assemble as representatives of an United nation? In a word, shall the American people in the plentitude of their strength be betrayed and vanquished by a disappointed faction, stripped of their forts and arsenals and find themselves suddenly without a capital and without a Government?" The *Tribune* announced on January 12 that what had happened was "a planned *coup d'etat.*" Greeley had issued a declaration of war and called upon all northerners to rally to the Republic's defense. Two days later the editor warned northern Democrats to recognize that either they would act like "loyal citizens" or be seen as "traitors."

From November 6, 1860, when he was elected president by a clear majority of electoral college votes, to March 4, 1861, when he was inaugurated, Abraham Lincoln, who had no power to direct the government and no clear direction to offer even if he could, did little more than observe southern states secede and form a government. For good or ill, right or wrong, the press described the president-elect in contradictory ways. In its varying ways it defined him, predicted what he would do, and either applauded or denounced him. The enemy that Jefferson Davis and his followers and most northern Democrats knew, for the most part, was the creation of newspaper imagery. He was also an enemy to be feared and despised.

Conversely, the Republican press presented readers with a new leader, whom they portrayed as strong, simple, and direct. He was a country lawyer, a man of the people chosen to defend the Republic against those bent on it destruction. Lincoln could be counted on to defend the Constitution and be fair but firm in dealings with southerners.

No inauguration speech rhetoric or public pronouncement that would follow would change either side's perception of who the new president was and who and what he represented. It was an environment in which neither Abraham Lincoln nor Jefferson Davis could formulate a policy or decide on a course of action that would back the country away from the brink of civil war. Given those circumstances, what happened on April 12, 1861, at Fort Sumter, South Carolina, was well-nigh inevitable.

7 Firing on Fort Sumter: A Republic at War with Itself

Less than a week after news of Lincoln's election, the South Carolina legislature, in a unanimous vote, instructed that a state convention be held. The purpose was to pass a resolution that would take the state out of the Union. On December 20, 1860, the resolution was approved. Four days later, the delegates published a list of reasons for their action. They cited northern hostility toward slavery and emphasized that the president-elect had received support from only one section of the country and so, in their eyes, could not claim to lead all of the country.

By February 1, 1861, more than a month before Inauguration Day, the seven states that composed the Lower South, one by one, left the Union. On February 9, delegates representing each of those states formed the Confederacy and chose Jefferson Davis to lead it. Davis chose February 23, Washington's birthday, for his inauguration. Attempts both by the now lame-duck President James Buchanan and by Kentucky senator John Crittenden to find a way to repair the damage to the Union were to no avail. Neither President-elect Lincoln nor most in his party offered support for yet another effort to compromise. When, on March 4, 1864, Abraham Lincoln took the oath of office he assumed leadership of a divided nation.

In his first inaugural address, Abraham Lincoln pleaded with fellow citizens, in particular with those in the Lower South, for reconciliation, but the incoming president offered no compromise that might result in reunifying the divided country. Pleas for reconciliation aside, Lincoln's key concerns were the future of the slaveholding states that were still in the Union and whether, if persuasion failed, force should be used to restore federal authority in areas that—as Lincoln and many northerners saw it—were in a state of rebellion.

The immediate issue that led to armed conflict was the presence of federal troops within the borders of states that had seceded. Although the number of those troops was too small to constitute a threat, President Jefferson Davis had to decide whether his new confederacy, now constituted as a sovereign nation, could allow any foreign troops on its soil. Lincoln had to consider whether removing those troops would constitute de facto recognition of the Confederacy as a legitimate government. The federal president also had to calculate whether, if left in place, those troops would be attacked. The answer to such agonizing questions came at Fort Sumter, located on an island in sight of Charleston, South Carolina. Davis, convinced that federal troops had to be removed and by then also sure that they would not be, ordered bombardment of the fort. With Lincoln unwilling to escalate the conflict by attempting to reinforce the garrison, and because of bad weather unable to re-supply it, surrender came quickly and without casualties.[1]

The Fort Sumter incident dramatically changed the dialogue about national separation within both regions. Contentions shifted to considering the steps necessary on one side to bring about a permanent division of the country and on the other side to prevent that division. As with other episodes, the press informed people what had happened at Fort Sumter and offered explanations of why it happened. As in past instances, press rhetoric served to inflame passions, as descriptions of cannon-fire—either justifiable or unjustifiable cannon-fire—were sure to do. Whatever their positions, editors played fast and loose with facts and logic. The attack on Fort Sumter, and the way in which newspapers presented the story and explained its implications, hardened opposition to compromise, reinforcing the fear and hostility of the people in one region toward those in the other. Examining newspaper accounts of the crisis before the attack and then after it, it is evident that the Fort Sumter incident represented for the people of both regions a passing of the point of no return in the march away from reconciliation and toward civil war.

In an editorial that typified the position of northern Democratic newspapers before the attack, the Providence, Rhode Island, *Daily Post* insisted that northerners, still hoping the southern states that had seceded would rejoin the Union, would never engage in a civil war to coerce southern people to reunite with them. The *Daily Post,* which had supported Douglas in 1860, asked on February 3, 1861, "'Will they [northern people] consent to a dissolution of the Union, and a Civil War, merely to please the crazy fanatics who have managed this anti-slavery agitation? Will they make the Negro their god, and give up their natural greatness, their prosperity—their name—their firesides—

everything for which, as a people, they have been proud—for the sake of worshiping according to the creed of Wendell Phillips? We warn the fanatics that they will not do it.'"[2]

In the same vein, on March 8, 1861, the New York *Herald* carried the terse if despicable comment that "'nigger worship has ruined churches, ruined parties and now is ruining the whole country.'"[3] The editorial followed with the assertion that slave labor was treated better than white labor. Surely there was no point in a war over slavery. Even a Republican newspaper, the Hartford, Connecticut, *Daily Times,* writing on April 12, 1861, the day that first reports arrived of the attack on Fort Sumter, insisted that the public favored "'recognizing the Confederacy. We are willing,'" the *Times* added, "'that they should go their own way, and solve by experiment the problem whether a republic built on slavery as its corner stone, can thrive and hold an honorable place among nations.'"[4] For every northern newspaper that did not see war as the logical outcome of secession, many more did predict that outcome or at least they rejected any effort to avoid it.

For most Republican newspapers, the lesson learned from secession was that the more southern slaveholders became a minority the more convinced they were that the majority endangered their security and interests. With that in mind, readers were told that the more southerners felt threatened the more they would use the threat of secession to get what they wanted. Republican editors reminded readers that in 1832 Jackson had stood firm against South Carolina and faced down the secessionist threat. As the editors saw it, compromise with the "slaveocracy" only encouraged slaveholders' intransigence and their demands for more and more control. Standing firm had saved the Republic before, so why not again?

Whatever the reasons for it, the attack on Fort Sumter provided the spark that ignited the powder keg. For all intents and purposes the incident ended hope of the Union being saved without use of force. It became clear that the seceding states would never agree to rejoin the Union without coercion; moreover, it was likely, if not yet certain, that the federal government would not allow the sundering of the Union without a struggle. Did Jefferson Davis and his colleagues intend Fort Sumter to be the defining moment, perhaps as the key to bringing the eight slave states that had yet to secede into the Confederacy, or did Abraham Lincoln seek to confront the Confederacy as a means of unifying both his party and the northern public in general? Historians have struggled with those questions for generations and still have no definitive answers. What is clear is that whatever the reasons for the actions taken, four of the eight slave states remaining in the Union joined the Confederacy within forty-eight hours after the attack on Fort Sumter. In the North, where Democrats and Republicans disagreed over who had brought the Republic to the point where a portion of its people had deserted it, the firing on American soldiers and their flag also had a unifying effect.

Publishing two weeks before the cannons fired and with rumors circulating of Lincoln's determination to defend both Fort Sumter and Fort Pickens in Florida, on April 1 the Republican St. Louis *Missouri Democrat* scornfully described the newly formed Confederacy and its leaders. The editor assured readers that although Lincoln was for peace, the disunionists were for war. Moreover, Lincoln was the defender of the American heritage, whereas the disunionists mocked it. Referring to the Confederacy's repeal of the Constitution and replacing it with one of their own making, the newspaper warned that the Confederacy's leaders "have come to regard Washington, Jefferson, Adams, Madison, Hamilton and the rest as shallow sentimental politicians whose work, admired as it has been by the enlightened world, and worshiped by the purist spirits of the Nineteenth Century, must be utterly abolished by the present generation." The newspaper pressed the point by writing that "the old tenants of the nation's Pantheon are thus unceremoniously ejected and in place of them given the vulpine visage of Slidell [John Slidell of Louisiana, a leading southern Democrat] and the sardonic countenance of [Jefferson] Davis."

On April 15, the day the report of the attack on Fort Sumter appeared in the *Democrat,* the newspaper expressed no surprise. This firing on the American flag, this ultimate act of treason, it told readers, was thirty years in the making and entirely the work of southern secessionists. Admonishing the federal government to stand up for the Republic, the *Democrat* insisted that "the Government can't allow itself to be awed by traitors."

Writing on April 9, a few days before the attack and with news of ships being sent to re-provision Fort Sumter, the Chicago *Tribune* expressed a defiant view of the South Carolinians and the Confederacy in general, a view shared by other Republican newspapers. In reply to reports that South Carolina would attack supply ships, the editor declared, "He who is not willing to do service under the old flag is already a recruit under the rattlesnake banner. Now for a quick contest and speedy peace." The newspaper anticipated that southern demands would be such that the North could not accept them. It was a matter of the South backing away or there would be war. On April 13, with news of the firing on the fort, the *Tribune* explained the attack as the result of a minority who, having lost an election, resorted to "rule by force." The editor advised, "We must defend the Union and the Constitution no matter how long it takes."

The Republican press hammered at the theme that the Republic had been attacked and that the attackers, moved by evil motives, were engaged in acts of treason. The time to compromise had passed, and patriots must rally to the defense of their country. The Indianapolis *Journal* declared on April 10 that the seceded states wanted war and were bent on destroying what the Founders had created. The *Journal* labeled South Carolinians as Tories, "as mean, as spiritless and false as ever disgraced the Revolution," a charge reminiscent of Charles Summer's rhetoric. The piece concluded by referring to the Confederacy as "the government of Jeff Davis versus the government of George Washington." On April 13, the day before news came of the attack on Fort Sumter, the *Journal* linked "the Tories to Democrats more concerned with their party than their country," and, having received news of the attack, the next day the editor declared that "to make peace would cost us some of our manhood, patriotism, and place in world opinion."

On the day after the surrender at Fort Sumter, Horace Greeley's New York *Tribune* proclaimed that "Fort Sumter is lost but Freedom is saved." Greeley scornfully speculated about what he labeled the "pro southern northern papers" would say now and concluded that "treason has occurred."[5] Over the next several days the *Tribune* denounced the actions of the South, attributing them to the power over the southern people of "the slave power conspiracy." In further attacks on northern Democrats the newspaper called for partisan political positions to be laid aside.[6] After all, Greeley insisted, while the North sought compromise the South planned treason.

Jefferson Davis miscalculated if he expected northern Democratic newspapers to continue to be sympathetic to the southern cause and to denounce the Black Republicans. Right up to the attack on Fort Sumter, the New York *Herald* had been blasting the Republican administration, denouncing it as "sacrificing the welfare of the land, and betraying its most sacred interests."[7] But on April 13, with the telegraphed reports of the attack in hand, James Gordon Bennett turned on the Confederacy and for the first time laid all blame at the door of the South. Bennett doubtless saw that a change of stance was needed to keep his newspaper offices from being mobbed, burned, or both. "'The Disunion conspiracy which has for the last twenty years been gnawing at the heart-strings of the great American republic,'" the *Herald* declared, "'has at last culminated in open war upon its glittering and resplendent flag. For the first time in the history of the United States, an organized attempt is made to destroy, by force of arms, the government which the American people have formed for themselves—to overthrow the glorious Constitution which has made us the envy of the world.'"[8] The angry editorial concluded by informing readers that the federal government had taken more than it should in insults and demands from the South. It was time to stop asking what might have been done, to set aside party differences, and to unite in the search for peace. As for the South, the *Herald* concluded that southern fire-eaters had won control of public opinion.

The Democratic and strongly pro-southern Cincinnati *Enquirer,* which up to the firing on Fort Sumter had laid blame for secession and the impending conflict on the abolitionist conspirators who wanted all slave states out of the Union, on April 13 told readers that it hoped that the guns would "awaken people North and South to the danger of war." Compromise was still possible, the editor suggested, but he made clear that southerners were the aggressors. "They broke the status quo" and so would "receive the indignant condemnation of every patriot." Over the next few days the *Enquirer* called on Democrats to join with Republicans to support the Union and pursue the war. The editor concluded that "Confederates must see that the North is not divided."[9]

While the attack on Fort Sumter had rallied northerners to the common cause of defending the Republic, it unified southerners as well in that same cause. Border states were forced off the fence by pressure from both sides. Virginia joined the Confederacy, and three other slaveholding border states followed; Arkansas, North Carolina, and Tennessee. Those remaining wavered but stayed in the Union. The southern press responded in kind to shouts of "Tories," "traitors," "monarchists," and more that emanated from the northern press. From its perspective it was the North, led by Black Republicans and abolitionists, that sacrificed the Union, deserted the republican principles of the Founding Fathers, disobeyed the law, and threatened anarchy.

In its April 11 issue the unionist Memphis *Appeal,* which as late as April 3 was denouncing extremists on both sides, carried the headline "Lincoln Urges War against the South." Reacting to the administration's refusal to abandon Fort Sumter, the newspaper declared the Republican president and his party untrustworthy and denounced both. "The chosen chief of an infidel and agrarian horde of Black Republicans who have usurped the Constitution and established a central despotism upon its ruins, now demands the implicit obedience of a free and sovereign people who, by virtue of their untrammeled will have established a new Government to which they render a cheerful allegiance." The *Appeal* referred to the Lincoln administration as "a cabal seeking war," insisting that it was northern fanatics who forced the South to secede and that those same fanatics would force blood to be spilled. Lincoln, the newspaper declared, "is a despot while the South defends liberty."

Two days later, on April 13, the report of the attack in hand, the *Appeal* attributed what had happened to "the treachery of the Lincoln Administration" and in dramatic words announced that "the northern Goths will be united in their unholy crusade upon the fair daughters and brave men of the South."

The New Orleans *Bee* argued that Lincoln's refusal to abandon the southern forts revealed his intention to provoke an attack. In less similar language to that of the *Appeal,* the *Bee* warned that the South needed to defend herself against "the frenzied hosts of Northern Abolitionists."[10] Two days before the attack, and after reiterating its position that all the South was doing was defending itself, the newspaper announced to northerners that the South was willing to go to war rather than consider rejoining a union of which abolitionists were a part. On April 15, after reporting the fall of Fort Sumter, the editor noted that the attack had united the South.

The Savannah *Morning News,* striking an even more militant pose, told readers that Lincoln would be whipped if he insisted on fighting. When Maj. Robert Anderson, commander of the small federal garrison at Fort Sumter, surrendered, the *News* rejoiced both at the victory and at the fact that no lives had been lost. In describing a victory celebration in Savannah, the editor reported that "even the Negroes gave expression to their satisfaction at the results of the first battle with Abe Lincoln's forces."[11]

From Charleston itself, the *Courier* provided both an impassioned account of events in its city and its opinion about what they meant for the Confederacy. On April 2, with the demand that the federal troops leave Fort Sumter having been made and with much speculation as to how the Lincoln administration would respond, the newspaper announced that whatever Lincoln did would reflect his partisan interest in building the Republican Party and not the best interest of the country. Two days later, after reporting the adoption of a constitution for the Confederacy, the editor observed, "If we are true to ourselves and our destiny, we have ample elements and resources of defense, protection, progressive developments, and Republican empire in the States that have seceded." This undoubtedly was a response to those northern editors who had questioned the Confederacy's ability to stand on its own, economically and militarily, and to their charges that the Confederacy would be a tyrannical government.

On April 12, before the firing began, the newspaper warned that the federal government was gathering troops in Washington, presumably for the purpose of attacking the Confederacy. The editor assured that "no knees are trembling and no faces are blushed with fear." After declaring an attack on the fort to be imminent, the *Courier* insisted that "honor is dearer than life to South Carolinians." The next morning, April 13, the *Courier's* headline read "Hostilities Commenced." What followed was the editor's summation and explanation of how that had come to pass:

> The sword must cut asunder the last tie that bound us to a people [the northerners] whom, in spite of wrongs and injustice was only indicted through a

long series of years, we had not yet utterly hated and despised. The last expiring spark of affection must be quenched in blood. Some of the most splendid pages in our glorious history must be blurred. A blow must be struck that would make the ears of every Republican fanatic tingle, and whose dreadful effects will be felt by generations yet to come. We must transmit a heritage of rankling and undying hate to our children.

All of this, the *Courier* instructed readers, was the product of "the treachery of our enemy." It was with God's blessing to have "turned our backs forever upon our former brothers."

In an editorial a week after the bombardment and subsequent fall of Fort Sumter, a pro-confederacy newspaper in slave state Missouri—which had not seceded—insisted that "'the States are the true guardians of our freedom and our rights, and when their power is gone, the master at the Federal Capital is the ruler over subject millions—an emperor.'"[12] On April 15 the New Orleans *Bee* declared that the North's claim to be fighting to preserve the Union was a lie and that, in fact, northerners were fighting to "subjugate the South." The word *subjugate* would appear often in the southern press in the weeks ahead.

Each side thus made its case for fighting to preserve the republican principle of freedom as ensured in individual and states' rights. The press of each region declared confidence that readers would defend the Republic and the heritage of the Founding Fathers, which, each declared, the other side sought to destroy.

Throughout these events the Washington, D.C., *National Intelligencer* stood firm in its support for "Liberty and Union." As late as April 9, three days before the attack, the *Intelligencer* called for the federal government to offer southern people a course of action as an alternative to that of the Confederacy. The editor demanded that the federal government squarely face the issue of secession and find a solution to the problems that provoked it. The newspaper urged a convention of all non-seceding states. At that event the Constitution would be "revised in ways to get restoration of the Union and while it [the convention] goes on, to keep the South from attacking any federal forts."

Four days later, the reports from Charleston in hand, the *Intelligencer* despaired over what had happened. In a brief report of the outbreak of hostilities the editor declared, "We can only give expression to the profound sorrow with which we contemplate the melancholy spectacle of a fratricidal conflict which, however begun can bring only shame to every lover of his land, and only grief to every friend of humanity."[13] The following day the newspaper criticized the actions of the federal and Confederate governments, noting that at least there were no casualties in the Fort Sumter action. It expressed hope that matters could still be resolved without resorting to war.

On April 16, now focusing on the impending decision in Virginia about whether to secede, the *Intelligencer* fixed blame for what had happened on the South and insisted that southerners had no good excuse for what it labeled "an ignoble war; ignoble because inspired in its origin by no generous ideas, and impelled by no civil necessity save that which is the outgrowth of human passions." The editor declared South Carolina to be the culprit in this crime. It was because of that one state that "the foundations of government laid by Washington, Madison and Jefferson [all Virginians] are to be overturned and the land of peace and plenty to be drenched in blood." Analyzing how things had come to such a pass, the *Intelligencer* blamed secessionists and declared that it was the North's reaction to those fire-eaters that had brought Republicans to power. It also argued that southern apprehension as to what a Republican president might do was no reason to destroy the Republic that the people had created. Earlier, the *Intelligencer* had criticized the role of northern and southern politicians and—by extension—the press in inflaming passions. Now this sober newspaper, so long tied to the Union, argued that but for these passions, inspired by whatever sources, war might have been averted.

As with each of the events but more dramatically than any of the others, reports of the firing on Fort Sumter paradoxically dissolved differences among people within each region and dramatized their differences. The first true battle between opposing armies would not occur for more than three months and newspapers such as the *National Intelligencer* would still urge compromise, but positions had hardened to the point where no compromise was possible. Fort Sumter represented the disintegration of a single community that had many common values and a shared political culture. The conflict represented not only the rejection of that culture but also each side's belief that the other side, bent on destroying it, had to be stopped. The tragic irony was that the cause for which each fought was the same, and yet they fought. Urged on by newspapers, some elements in the American community came to believe other elements in that same community conspired to subvert its values and destroy it.

In the roughly three months between the attack on Fort Sumter and the first all-out clash of armies, the press throughout the increasingly divided country sought to define the conflict and vindicate its cause, whether it be that of the federal union or the Confederate states. The argument was described as fundamentally one between friends and foes of the Republic. For the southern press, the revolutionaries were justified by the actions of a government that would deny them constitutionally protected rights and liberties. That press frequently alluded to the American Revolution, placing southerners in the role of revolutionary patriots and northerners and their president in the role of British oppressors.

Almost without exception, the northern press framed the conflict in terms of the loyalty of northerners to the Republic and the heritage of the Founders and the disloyalty of southerners, who, for their own self-interested reasons, had taken up arms and by so doing rejected their heritage. If the northern press agreed in projecting a sense of betrayal of the American heritage on the part of the South, northern newspapers remained at odds over how to respond to the act of betrayal. Should the federal government use force and so coerce the seceded states, or should it peacefully let them go? Even after the firing on Fort Sumter, some argued for a peaceful dissolution of the Union. Shots fired in anger provoked anger, however, and the weight of press opinion clearly was on the side of using force. It was described as the patriotic response to treasonous acts. Some of the northern press even claimed that war would be a blessing and the salvation of republican virtues that had slipped away during the years of economic growth, when too many men worshiped wealth instead of commonwealth. Whether war was a positive good or a necessary evil, the northern press recognized the need to act to put down a rebellion.

The Boston *Herald,* a Democratic publication that had supported Douglas in the election of 1860, editorialized on April 15 that "'the right of the people to self-government is too precious a boon to be overthrown by a revolution having for its object a reign of despotism and a total disregard for the people.'" The editor made clear that "'a slave owner is naturally overbearing and despotic.'"[14] After denouncing both abolitionist fanatics and southern fire-eaters for their incendiary behavior, the *Herald* lectured readers that "men must perform their duty to defend the Republic created by the Fathers." The editorial concluded with the call to defend the country's honor.

The Republican New York *Times* also considered honor to be at stake. In an April 15 editorial it dismissed arguments that the Confederates acted like the revolutionaries of 1776 or that they legitimately could claim the role of defenders of the Republic. The *Times* rejected the southern editors' argument that civil war was consistent with republican rights and argued instead that it was contrary to the theory of the Republic. The *Times* insisted that the framers of the Constitution, by providing a means for lawful protest and legitimate ways of determining who shall have power, had made any future revolution unnecessary and illegitimate. The piece concluded with the assertion that southern action represented not revolution but conspiracy and treason.

In the same vein, in the wake of the attack on Fort Sumter the Boston *Post,* which had supported John C. Breckenridge, on April 16 declared to readers who had to this point been sympathetic to the South that South Carolina's action was "'false to the first principles of Republican Government.'" The newspaper then insisted that "'there is left no choice but between a support of the Government and anarchy.'" Republican government, "'the world's best hope,'" was threatened, as was the heritage of the Founding Fathers.[15]

Although the sentiments of these newspapers were typical of what one read in the northern press in the days, weeks, and months after the attack, patriotism did not blot out politics entirely. The pro-Douglas Detroit *Free Press,* after describing a North in "'a vast upheaval of courage, patriotism, and devotion to the best interests of the nation,'" made clear that the upheaval concerned rallying around the Constitution rather than Abraham Lincoln and his party.[16] After chiding southerners for the act that now made it impossible for conservative northerners to continue to seek compromise with them, the New York *Journal of Commerce,* which had urged the election of Breckenridge, warned that northern conservatives now must turn their attention to protecting the Constitution. The editor reminded southerners that "'a state of war supposes but two classes of people—friends and foes'" and that to support the South now would be treason.[17] Having so declared loyalty to the Union, the newspaper made clear its belief that matters had reached this point because of "'the blunders and the pernicious principles of the dominant party.'"[18]

There were occasional calls for reconciliation, for a peace conference, or for respecting the motives, if not applauding the actions, of southerners. Republican newspapers and a good deal of the northern Democratic press, however, viewed the southern acts as treasonable and called for northerners to rise to the defense of the Republic.

Having earlier made clear that the war to come was about the defense of the Republic and not about the end of slavery, Horace Greeley's New York *Tribune* insisted in an April 25 editorial that a war for the Republic would result in a "national regeneration." The formerly pro-Breckenridge Columbus, Ohio, *Daily Capitol City Fact* in a May 18 editorial denounced the "'Slave Oligarchy that demanded the surrender of northern rights, northern honor, northern self-respect.'"[19] The words *integrity, honor,* and *self-respect* often appeared in much of the northern press. Readers were challenged to show manliness and selflessness in defending the heritage of the Founding Fathers against the threats from southern traitors.

For some of the northern press the portrayal of the nobility of the northern cause, and the societal good that would come of it, was carried even further. In an April 20 editorial, the Republican Springfield, Massachusetts, *Republican* preached that men had grown mad for money, but "'war has broken up the nightmare of commerce.'" Now young men could "'feel the genuine thrill of patriotism. . . . Verily war is a means of grace to them . . . party names are wiped out and for once in fifty years men stand together as patriots.'" The editor concluded by assuring readers that "'honorable war is better than corrupt peace.'"[20] The Providence, Rhode Island, *Journal,* also Republican, observed that "'it is a piece of good fortune to be a young man now and here. It is time for sacrifice and so a time for heroism. At no period in this country's history, since the revolution, . . . has it been so glorious and joyful to have a life to give.'"[21] The words *regeneration* and *rededication* conjured up the image of heroism for this generation. It was the North not the South that was to be engaged in a second American Revolution that would be dedicated to saving the Republic and rededicating its people to republican principles. By so doing, this generation would be saved from selling its soul for gold and silver.

The usually cynical New York *Herald* editorialized on April 29 that "without war and the suffering it entails men would degenerate. Without war patriotism and heroism would die out from want of food. Without war society would become steeped in luxury and effeminacy." The newspaper concluded by insisting that "the chief cause of the present war is excessive prosperity" and that "the effect of this war will be to purge party politics and its corruptions, and the country will come out of the fire like gold purified of its dross, better and brighter than ever." The Boston *Transcript* called it "'a holy war,'" and Weed's Albany *Evening Journal* proclaimed that it would uplift the moral character of the people.[22]

The firing on Fort Sumter made the position of northern conservatives all but untenable. It had the same result for southern unionists. How could one call for loyalty to a government that had called up an army of some seventy-five thousand men ostensibly bent on the invasion of the South and the subjugation of its people? The Louisville *Courier* described the situation after Fort Sumter as many southern newspapers would describe it. It declared Lincoln's actions to be "'a war for the enslavement of the people of the South.'" The editor noted that all slave states had a common cause, which he described as "'to maintain her sovereignty, to defend the rights of her citizens and to preserve their liberties.'"[23] These were all good republican principles.

As the majority of the southern press saw matters after the Fort Sumter incident, which they portrayed as an act to defend South Carolina's sovereignty and protect its citizenry, Lincoln, by calling for volunteers, had acted aggressively and provocatively toward the South. Some publications insisted that he had acted unconstitutionally. Those newspapers declared that Lincoln and his party had denied southerners their rights as Americans in the same way that their ancestors had been denied their rights as English. Just as the English king had forfeited his right to the loyalty of American colonists, the American president had forfeited his right to demand loyalty from southerners. As the southern press described it, the South had not abandoned the Republic or renounced the heritage of the Founding Fathers. The Republicans had done that. Southern newspapers told readers that they must fight to protect the Republic and save it from those who would destroy it. They must fight for the sake of saving what their revolutionary forefathers had created and bequeathed to them. They were embarked on the course of the second American Revolution. Fort Sumter had been their version of Lexington and Concord.

A week after the attack, the pro-southern St. Louis *Republican* declared Lincoln's response to be a northern Republican effort to crush liberty in the South. The editor made the analogy to the Revolution and described the states and not the federal government as "the true guardians of our freedom and our rights."[24] What was at stake was "'our and our children's freedom—a question whether our liberties are secured by laws or whether they are subject to the will, the mere will of despotism.'" In North Carolina, after making clear its earlier support for the Constitutional Union Party, the Raleigh *Standard* acknowledged on April 20 that revolution was upon the nation and declared itself unable to support a government bent on subjugating the South.[25] In Tennessee, the Nashville *Daily Patriot* declared "'war in defense of freedom'" and noted that southerners had the right of revolution.[26] The New Orleans *Bee* scoffed at the northern claim that it was to be a war for the Union. On April 15 the editor rhetorically asked how a union based upon republican principles could use force to keep the South as part of it.

As for Lincoln's promise to protect southern rights, in particular its institution of slavery, many newspapers declared that his actions had proven he could not be trusted. On May 9 the Nashville *Republican Banner* used the sort of language characteristic of the press in all regions throughout these years of crisis. The editor declared, "We repudiate and scorn and spit upon the men and the spirit by whom and by which the best government the world ever saw has been perverted into an engine of oppression to one half of its people, because they held an institution, recognized in the fundamental law, obnoxious to these Union savers." This was not secession but revolution, and revolution was "an inherent and inalienable right." It concluded with the declaration that this government "had forfeited its right to govern."[27]

As the press presented it, the attack on Fort Sumter provided the final evidence that persuaded northerners to believe that southerners had become converts to the treasonous ways of the fire-eaters. As the southern press described that event and Lincoln's response to it, southerners were convinced that northerners had become converts to the fanatical ways of the abolitionists. In the face of those beliefs one republic became two, and the dismembered pieces fell into fratricidal war for the sake of preserving the same principles. In the wake of Fort Sumter neither Davis nor Lincoln could find a way to change course. As for the newspapers, once again both the positions they took, and the language they used in taking them, reflected and in ways impossible to measure influenced their readers' thoughts and feelings, all in defense of "the Republic." The outbreak of the Civil War was grimly ironic. Over the next four years this deadly irony cost more than six hundred thousand lives.

CONCLUSION: THE SHATTERED REPUBLIC

From the moment of independence, Americans faced the daunting task of creating what Benedict Anderson has called "an imagined community."[1] Could people with different religious beliefs and who came from different ethnic backgrounds, were divided by class differences, and lived in communities far apart both in time and space be able to find some common identity? Lacking the bonds that one religion, one heritage, or at least the familiarity that came with social interaction that might be formed, Americans found communal bonds in ideas, images, myths, and symbols that reflected a shared belief and agreed-upon values in what they called republican society. From the Revolution to the Civil War, that culture was the centripetal force that held the American community together. But in the spring of 1861 centrifugal forces won out, and the imagined American community was shattered.[2]

The causes of division were complex but may be summed up as fear on the part of rival groups within that community that their enemy would undermine republican society and destroy the bonds that held the community together. What happened in the last years before the Civil War was high drama, and the press made the most of it in telling the story of crisis upon crisis. As Walter Lippmann said of public opinion, it amounts to pictures in people's heads.[3] Words in the press provided the outlines and much of the coloration for those pictures. Whatever slant a newspaper used in describing and interpreting an event; however the press portrayed the key actors, America's newspapers were playing the role of both messenger and participant. To what extent newspapers were the latter we can only speculate, but that they played such a role—that for whatever reasons they influenced what happened—seems certain.

Given what appeared in the southern and northern Democratic press, it is not surprising that no matter how often Lincoln and other Republican leaders insisted that they had no intention of disturbing slavery where it already existed, and that they offered no more threat to southern society than had George Washington, many southerners came to believe that Republicans were all like John Brown. These southerners became convinced that abolitionists, whom they equated with Republicans, would end slavery everywhere and by the most uncivilized of means if that was what it took to attain their nefarious goal. Similarly, no matter how often and vociferously Illinois Sen. Stephen A. Douglas and his supporters insisted that his goal and his party's was the preservation of the Union and not the protection of slaveholders, many northerners would not believe them.

Readers of some northern newspapers encountered images of southerners as bullies who were prone to violence, disrespectful of laws, and manipulators of the Constitution to suit their interests. Those who claimed to be chivalrous in fact were perceived to be dishonorable. Eventually, most northern newspapers came to portray all southerners as a conspiratorial, immoral element of society intent on destroying the Republic for the sake of keeping their slave property. Those newspapers insisted that southerners could not be trusted and that anyone who did was either naive, frightened, or so politically motivated as to put office-holding above any principle. It became easy to believe that southern fire-eaters had intimidated President Buchanan and those who supported him.

Given the degree to which each side saw the other as the Republic's enemy, it became impossible to accept the other side as a legitimate political opponent to whom political power could be entrusted. The very basis of republican society had been undermined. We can only wonder what might have happened had the press been fairer, more balanced, and less strident in describing and explaining events as well as characterizing key figures and whole segments of society. Newspapers, strutting and posturing, chose to exaggerate in order to excite the passions of readers. Although the reasons for such heightened rhetoric are hard to know, straining for competitive advantage doubtless was part of it, as were the too-human emotions that journalists engendered in readers and, perhaps, in themselves. As the great twentieth-century journalist Eric Sevareid once observed, it is impossible to shout and tell the truth at the same time.

Writing about the role of media in building imagined communities, Michael Ignatieff has pointed out that the media could also be used to divide those communities. He contended that "the media now play the decisive role in constituting the imagined community of nation and globe, the myth that millions of separable 'I's' find common identity in a 'we.'" He further argued that the media can also bring to life "local nationalizing" and as a consequence help create conditions that lead to the destruction of the broader imagined community.[4] Although newspapers on the eve of the American Civil War could not compare with today's mass media in ability to reach their audiences, the press at mid-century offered messages with fewer distractions, without satellite dishes full of competing words and images. The press by the mid-nineteenth century was in a position to influence mass thinking as never before. Newspapers did indeed contribute mightily to the shaping of an imagined community and, ironically, to the shattering of that community.

NOTES

Preface

1. Michael Morrison, *Slavery and the American West: The Eclipse of Manifest Destiny and the Coming of the Civil War* (Chapel Hill: University of North Carolina Press, 1997), 7.

2. Susan-Mary Grant, *North over South: Northern Nationalism and American Identity in the Antebellum Era* (Lawrence: University of Kansas Press, 2000), 28.

3. Jonathan Adkins, *Parties, Politics, and the Sectional Conflict in Tennessee, 1823-1861* (Knoxville: University of Tennessee Press, 1997), 259, emphasis in the original.

4. James M. McPherson, *What They Fought For, 1861-1865* (Baton Rouge: Louisiana State University Press, 1994), 6; James McPherson, *For Cause and Comrades: Why Men Fought in the Civil War* (New York: Oxford University Press, 1997), passim.

Introduction

1. Abraham Lincoln, "First Inaugural Address, Mar. 4, 1861," in Abraham Lincoln, *The Essential Abraham Lincoln,* ed. John Gabriel Hunt (Avenal, N.J.: Gramercy Books, 1993), 222.

2. Lincoln, *The Essential Lincoln,* 219.

Chapter 1: The Emergence of a Democratic Press

1. The Louisiana Purchase of 1803, surely the greatest $15 million bargain ever, provided enormous unexploited resources. Eventually, thirteen states were created from the Louisiana Territory: Arkansas, Colorado, Iowa, Kansas, Louisiana, Minnesota, Missouri, Montana, Nebraska, North Dakota, Oklahoma, South Dakota, and Wyoming.

2. Gerald Baldasty, *The Commercialization of News in the Nineteenth Century* (Madison: University of Wisconsin Press, 1992).

3. Frank Luther Mott, *American Journalism* (New York: Macmillan, 1941), 283, 285, 291.

4. William E. Huntzicker, *The Popular Press, 1833-1865* (Westport: Greenwood Press, 1999); Dan Schiller, *Objectivity and the News: The Public and the Rise of Commercial Journalism* (Philadelphia: University of Pennsylvania Press, 1981), passim.

5. Allan Pred, *Urban Growth and City-Systems in the United States, 1840–1860* (Cambridge: Harvard University Press, 1968), 222.

6. Pred, *Urban Growth and City-Systems,* citing, among other things, *Eighth Census, 1860, Mortality and Miscellaneous Statistics of the United States* (Washington: Government Printing Offfice, 1866); Alfred McClung Lee, *The Daily Newspaper in America: The Evolution of a Social Instrument* (New York: Macmillan, 1937), 718.

7. Willard G. Bleyer, *Main Currents in the History of American Journalism* (Boston: Houghton Mifflin, 1927), 158.

8. Bleyer, *Main Currents,* citing the *Public Ledger,* Mar. 27, Apr. 10, 1837.

9. Thomas Kiernan, *The Road to Colossus: A Celebration of American Ingenuity* (New York: William Morrow, 1985), 120.

10. Pred, *Urban Growth and City-Systems,* 146, and table A.41, 223.

11. Baldasty, *The Commercialization of News,* 5.

12. Ibid., citing Lee, *The Daily Newspaper in America,* 1167; Huntzicker, *The Popular Press,* 20.

13. Baldasty, *The Commercialization of News,* 44.

14. Bleyer, *Main Currents,* 204, quoting the New York *Herald,* Jan. 23, 1858.

15. Ibid., 204, quoting Samuel Bowles to the Springfield *Republican,* Dec. 9, 1859.

16. Lee, *The Daily Newspaper in America,* 197.

17. Richard Kielbowicz, *News in the Mail: The Press, Post Office, and Public Information, 1700–1860s* (Westport: Greenwood Press, 1989), 155.

18. Merrill Jensen, *The New Nation: A History of the United States during the Confederation, 1781–1789* (New York: Alfred A. Knopf, 1958), 430.

19. Kielbowicz, *News in the Mail,* 2.

20. Ibid., 3.

21. Bleyer, *Main Currents,* 224–26.

22. Lambert A. Wilmer, *Our Press Gang* (Philadelphia: J. T. Lloyd, 1859), quoted in Douglas Fermer, *James Gordon Bennett and the New York* Herald: *A Study in Editorial Opinion in the Civil War Era, 1854–1867* (New York: St. Martin's Press, 1986), 6.

23. Bleyer, *Main Currents,* 225, quoting James Ford Rhodes, "Newspapers as Historical Sources," in Rhodes, *Historical Essays* (1909, repr. Port Washington: Kennikat Press, 1966), 90–91.

24. Kielbowicz, *News in the Mail,* 152–53.

25. Ibid., 74, quoting Amos Kendall to the House Post Office Committee, House Report 909, 12. "The Postmaster General estimated that newspapers contributed 1.5 tons of each day's 2.0-ton shipment," Kielbowicz noted in an e-mail to Dwight L. Teeter Jr. on Feb. 13, 2001.

26. Richard Schwarzlose, *The Nation's Newsbrokers,* vol. 1: *The Formative Years, from Pre-Telegraph to 1865* (Evanston: Northwestern University Press, 1989), 25.

27. Pred, *Urban Growth and City-Systems,* 148–49.

28. Ibid., 45–47, maps 3.1, 3.2, 3.3, reworking "Railroads in Operation" maps from Charles O. Paullin, *Atlas of the Historical Geography of the United States* (Washington: Carnegie Institute and American Geographic Society, 1932), plates 138L, 139A, 139B.

29. Maury Klein, *Days of Defiance: Sumter, Secession, and the Coming of the Civil War* (New York: Alfred A. Knopf, 1997), 214.

30. Ibid.

31. Ibid., quoting Howard C. Perkins, *Northern Editorials on Secession* (Gloucester: Pe-

ter Smith, 1964), 2:1047–48. See also Louis M. Starr, *Bohemian Brigade: Civil War Newsmen in Action* (New York: Alfred A. Knopf, 1954), 9.

32. Henry David Thoreau, *The Annotated Walden: Walden; or Life in the Woods,* ed. Philip van Doren Stern (New York: Clarkson N. Potter, 1970), 188–89.

33. Fredericksburg *Herald* quoted in the Alexandria *Gazette,* Jan. 3, 1860, in Donald E. Reynolds, *Editors Make War: Southern Newspapers in the Secession Crisis* (Nashville: Vanderbilt University Press, 1970), 217.

34. Manufacturing accounted for "32 percent of the nation's commodity output by 1860." Pred, *Urban Growth and City-Systems,* 7.

35. New York *Sun,* May 27, 1844, quoted in Steven Smethers, "The Telegraph: A Revolutionary Force in U.S. Society," in *History of Mass Media in the United States: An Encyclopedia,* ed. Margaret A. Blanchard (Chicago: Fitzroy Dearborn, 1998), 635.

36. Pred, *Urban Growth and City-Systems,* 153.

37. Bleyer, *Main Currents,* 198, quoting Boston *Transcript,* Jan. 7, 1848.

38. Bleyer, *Main Currents,* 198, quoting New York *Herald,* June 11, 17, 1849.

39. Pred, *Urban Growth and City-Systems,* 153–54, see especially map 6.1.

40. Ibid., table A.47, 228.

41. We are indebted to C. Edward Caudill of the University of Tennessee for articulating these insights.

42. Pred, *Urban Growth and City-Systems,* 155.

43. Quoted in Schwarzlose, *The Nation's Newsbrokers,* 1:1, from the New York *Herald,* Feb. 19, 1846, emphasis in the original.

44. Klein notes, however, "None of the nation's 372 daily and 2,971 weekly papers in 1860 even approached the influence of the New York dailies. The rapid proliferation of telegraph wires not only spread and speeded up the flow of information but also allowed it to be centralized and dispersed like other commodities" (*Days of Defiance,* 214).

45. Schwarzlose, *The Nation's Newsbrokers,* 1:127.

46. Klein, *Days of Defiance,* 214.

47. Ibid., 213, 214.

48. Ibid., 213.

49. Kiernan, *The Road to Colossus;* Maury Klein, *The Flowering of the Third America: The Making of an Organizational Society, 1850–1920* (Chicago: Ivan R. Dee, 1993).

50. Ben H. Bagdikian, *The Media Monopoly,* 6th ed. (Boston: Beacon Press, 2000), passim.

51. New York *Herald,* May 12, 1845, quoted in Bleyer, *Main Currents,* 197–98.

52. Baldasty, *The Commercialization of News,* 8.

53. Hazel Dicken-Garcia, *Journalistic Standards in Nineteenth-Century America* (Madison: University of Wisconsin Press, 1989), 68.

54. Quoted in Klein, *Days of Defiance,* 25; see also Elizabeth Brown Dickey, "Robert Barnwell Rhett," in *Dictionary of Literary Biography,* vol. 43: *American Newspaper Journalists, 1690–1872,* ed. Perry J. Ashley (Detroit: Gale Research, 1985), 386–92.

55. Dicken-Garcia, *Journalistic Standards,* 107, 162, 182; Timothy W. Gleason, *The Watchdog Concept: The Press and the Courts in Nineteenth-Century America* (Ames: Iowa State University Press, 1990).

56. Jean Folkerts and Dwight L. Teeter, *Voices of a Nation: A History of Mass Media in the United States,* 3d ed. (Boston: Allyn and Bacon, 1998), 152.

57. Fermer, *James Gordon Bennett,* 37–38.

58. Gleason, *The Watchdog Concept,* 62–64.

59. James Morton Smith, *Freedom's Fetters: The Alien and Sedition Laws and American Civil Liberties* (Ithaca: Cornell University Press, 1956), chs. 2 and 6.

60. Norman L. Rosenberg, *Protecting the Best Men: An Interpretive History of the Law of Libel* (Chapel Hill: University of North Carolina Press, 1986), 105.

61. Rosenberg (*Protecting the Best Men,* 107) discusses the example of James Cheetham of the New York *American Citizen,* who in his first two years of publication was sued for libel thirteen times. William Duane, a Jeffersonian radical, also had to defend frequent suits. His opponents claimed that Duane's best libel defense would be that his reputation was so bad that his libels no longer hurt those he attacked.

62. Ibid., 132–33.

63. Ibid., 147–48, quoting Frederick Grimké, *The Nature and Tendency of Free Institutions,* ed. John William Ward (Cambridge: Harvard University Press, 1968), 398. Compare his sentiments to the marketplace-of-ideas philosophy in a dissenting opinion by Justice Holmes: *Abrams v. United States,* 250 U.S. 616, 629 (1919).

64. Harold L. Nelson, ed., *Freedom of the Press from Hamilton to the Warren Court* (Indianapolis: Bobbs-Merrill, 1967), 173–78 (for Virginia anti-abolition statutes passed in 1832, 1836, and 1848).

65. John C. Nerone, *Violence against the Press: Policing the Public Sphere in U.S. History* (New York: Oxford University Press, 1994), 9.

66. John Lofton, *The Press as Guardian of the First Amendment* (Columbia: University of South Carolina Press, 1980), 100–101; Nerone, *Violence against the Press,* 101–2.

67. Nerone, *Violence against the Press,* 97, quoting from "Mr. Birney's Answer," *The Philanthropist,* Jan. 1, 1836.

68. Nerone, *Violence against the Press,* 97, quoting Cincinnati *Whig,* Aug. 13, 1836. See also Lofton, *The Press as Guardian.*

69. Nerone, *Violence against the Press,* 105.

70. Lofton, *The Press as Guardian,* 93, quoting from the St. Louis *Missouri Argus,* Sept. 11, 1835.

71. Ibid., quoting from Lovejoy's St. Louis *Observer,* Oct. 11, 1835, and from Henry Tanner, *An Eye-Witness: An Account of the Life, Trials, and Perils of Rev. Elijah P. Lovejoy* (1881, repr. New York: A. M. Kelley, 1971), 55.

72. Lofton, *The Press as Guardian,* 94, quoting Tanner, *An Eye-Witness,* 60–61.

73. Lofton, *The Press as Guardian,* 95–96; Nerone, *Violence against the Press,* 105–7.

74. Nerone, *Violence against the Press,* 107–8; Lofton, *The Press as Guardian,* 98–101; Ronald T. Farrar, "Cassius Marcellus Clay," in *Dictionary of Literary Biography,* vol. 43: *American Newspaper Journalists, 1690–1872,* ed. Perry J. Ashley (Detroit: Gale Research, 1985), 98–102.

75. Lofton, *The Press as Guardian,* 99–100.

76. New York *Tribune,* June 25, 1849; H. Edward Richardson, *Cassius Marcellus Clay: Firebrand of Freedom* (Lexington: University Press of Kentucky, 1974), 50–55, 60–63, 60.

77. Nerone, *Violence against the Press,* 221–25, 226–30. Nerone reports that of 111 wartime mobbings, Ohio and Pennsylvania led the way with twenty-three and twenty-two, respectively. Indiana saw fourteen Civil War mobbings, and New York ten. For added support for the concept that mobbing was popular in mid-nineteenth-century America, see David Grimstead, *American Mobbing, 1828–1861: Toward Civil War* (New York: Oxford University Press, 1998).

78. Nerone, *Violence against the Press,* 225; Warren Francke, "James Gordon Bennett," in *Dictionary of American Literary Biography,* vol. 43: *American Newspaper Journalists, 1690–1872,* ed. Perry J. Ashley (Detroit: Gale Research, 1985), 41–42.

79. Folkerts and Teeter, *Voices of a Nation,* 153.

80. Bleyer, *Main Currents,* 158–61.

81. Piers Brendon, *The Life and Death of the Press Barons* (New York: Atheneum, 1983), 25.

82. Nickieann Fleener, "Benjamin Henry Day," in *Dictionary of American Literary Biography,* vol. 43: *American Newspaper Journalists, 1690–1872,* ed. Perry J. Ashley (Detroit: Gale Research, 1985), 136–38.

83. New York *Sun,* July 21, 1834, 12, reproduced in Bleyer, *Main Currents,* 159.

84. Bleyer, *Main Currents,* 159. Ironically, the correction appeared just above the following item: *"Charge of Libel:* On Friday afternoon a man named Thomas Fuller was brought before the police on complaint of Mr. Hutchings, in Chatham next door to Mott street, on a charge of having written and published a libel against Mr. Hutchings in the Democratic Chronicle, on the 2nd July, in relation that took place before his store door on the evening of July 1. Fuller was held to bail in the sum of $500 to appear and answer."

85. Ibid., 162; Edwin Emery and Michael Emery, *The Press and America,* 5th ed. (Englewood Cliffs: Prentice-Hall, 1984), 140–41.

86. New York *Sun,* Mar. 31, 1834, quoted in Bleyer, *Main Currents,* 160.

87. New York *Transcript,* June 23, 1834, quoted in Bleyer, *Main Currents,* 160–61.

88. John D. Stevens, *Sensationalism and the New York Press* (New York: Columbia University Press, 1991), 30–31.

89. New York *Herald,* July 3, Aug. 15, 20, 1845, quoted in Bleyer, *Main Currents,* 201.

90. Baldasty, *The Commercialization of News,* 44.

91. Ibid., citing William E. Ames, *A History of the* National Intelligencer (Chapel Hill: University of North Carolina Press, 1972), 239–41.

92. Fermer, *James Gordon Bennett,* 186.

93. New Orleans *Bee,* July 1, 1857.

Chapter 2: Impeding Civilization

1. For details of the episode, see David Donald, *Charles Sumner and the Coming of the Civil War* (New York: Alfred A. Knopf, 1960); for Brooks's own view of the matter, see Robert L. Meriweather, ed., "Preston Brooks and the Caning of Charles Sumner" in *South Carolina Historical and Genealogical Magazine* 52 (1951): 341–88.

2. Donald, *Charles Sumner and the Coming of the Civil War,* 223.

3. Ibid., 266.

4. Ibid., 290.

5. Newspapers of the time did not print cartoons or pictures of any sort, but some of the monthly magazines did. A portrayal of what happened appeared in *Harper's Weekly* with the caption "Southern Chivalry-Argument versus Club's."

6. Washington *National Daily Intelligencer,* May 23, 1856.

7. New York *Tribune,* May 24, 1856.

8. Ibid.

9. New York *Post,* May 23, 1856.

10. New York *Post,* May 30, 1856.

11. Albany *Evening Journal,* May 23, 1856.

12. Ibid.

13. Philadelphia *Ledger and Transcript,* May 24, 1856.

14. Boston *Transcript,* May 23, 1856.

15. Ibid.

16. Ibid.

17. Meriweather, ed., "Preston Brooks and the Caning of Charles Sumner," 2.

18. Preston Brooks to his brother, quoted in "Preston Brooks and the Caning of Charles Sumner," ed. Meriweather, 3.

19. Meriweather, ed., "Preston Brooks and the Caning of Charles Sumner," 1.

20. Ibid.

21. See especially Bertram Wyatt-Brown, *Southern Honor: Ethics and Behavior in the Old South* (New York: Oxford University Press, 1982). In *Yankee Saints and Southern Sinners* (Baton Rouge: Louisiana State University Press, 1985), Wyatt-Brown argues that although men of both regions were concerned with honor, they interpreted the issue differently. Grimsted observes that from 1835 onward, the South "invented a North without integrity or courage" (*American Mobbing, 1828–1861: Toward Civil War* [New York: Oxford University Press, 1998], 32). Our research supports the conclusion that both sides put great stock in honor as applied to each but found growing evidence that the other lacked that characteristic so important to the people of a republican society.

22. For good expositions of the thesis that such concerns (not the slavery issue) preoccupied Americans of the 1850s and produced a collapse of the second-party system, see Michael F. Holt, *Political Parties and American Political Development: From the Age of Jackson to the Age of Lincoln* (Baton Rouge: Louisiana State University Press, 1992), and Paul Kleppner, *The Third Electoral System, 1853–1892: Parties, Voters, and Political Cultures* (Chapel Hill: University of North Carolina Press, 1979).

23. Boston *Evening Transcript,* May 23, 1856.

24. New York *Courier and Enquirer,* May 23, 1856, quoted in the New York *Tribune,* May 28, 1856; New York *Times,* May 23, 1856.

25. New York *Tribune,* May 28, 1856.

26. Harold S. Schultz, *Nationalism and Sectionalism in South Carolina, 1852–1860* (Durham: Duke University Press, 1950), 23.

27. New York *Tribune,* May 31, 1856.

28. Ibid.

29. New York *Herald,* May 23, 1856.

30. New York *Herald,* May 24, 1856.

31. Cincinnati *Enquirer,* May 27, 1856.

32. St. Louis *Missouri Democrat,* May 29, 1856.

33. *Illinois State Register* (Springfield), May 26, 1856.

34. Louisville *Journal,* May 28, 1856.

35. Milledgeville *Federal Union,* June 3, 1856.

36. Greenville *Patriot and Mountaineer,* May 29, 1856.

37. Charleston *Courier,* May 28, 1856.

38. Charleston *Mercury,* May 24, 1856.

39. Richmond *Enquirer,* June 3, 1856.

40. Ibid.

Chapter 3: The Dred Scott *Decision and a Society of Laws*

1. For details of the case and its political and legal importance we have relied on Don E. Fehrenbacher's *The Dred Scott Case* (New York: Oxford University Press, 1978). For information about Roger Taney, see Carl Brent Swisher, *Roger B. Taney* (New York: Macmillan, 1935).

2. Swisher, *Taney*, 493.

3. For descriptions of Weed's early newspaper and political activities see Lorman Ratner, *Antimasonry: The Crusade and the Party* (Englewood Cliffs: Prentice-Hall, 1969); Paul Goodman, *Towards a Christian Republic: Antimasonry* (New York: Oxford University Press,1988); and Glyndon J. Van Deusen, *Thurlow Weed: Wizard of the Lobby* (Boston: Little Brown, 1947).

4. Albany *Evening Journal,* Mar. 9, 1857.

5. Ibid.

6. Ibid.

7. Washington *National Era,* Mar. 12, 1857.

8. Pittsburgh *Gazette,* Mar. 14, 1857.

9. Chicago *Tribune,* Mar. 11, 1857.

10. St. Louis *Missouri Democrat,* Mar. 13, 1857.

11. Augusta *Constitutionalist* quoted in Fehrenbacher, *The Dred Scott Case,* 418.

12. New York *Herald,* Mar. 15, 1857.

13. Ibid.

14. New York *Herald,* Mar. 12, 1857.

15. Memphis *Appeal,* Mar. 24, 1857.

16. New Orleans *Crescent,* Mar. 20, 1857.

17. Charleston *Mercury,* Mar. 17, 1857.

Chapter 4: Kansas and the Lecompton Constitution

1. Historians have long noted the importance of the Kansas conflict to the ultimate division of the Democratic Party and the growing sense of distrust on the part of people from one region toward those of another. See especially Michael Holt, *The Political Crisis of the 1850s* (New York: John Wiley, 1978), and Michael Holt, *Political Parties and American Political Development* (Baton Rouge: Louisiana State University Press, 1992). See also Kenneth Stampp, *The Imperiled Union: Essays on the Background of the Civil War* (New York: Oxford Unviersity Press, 1980); William Gienapp, "The Republican Party and the Slave Power," in *New Perspectives on Race and Slavery in America: Essays in Honor of Kenneth M. Stampp,* ed. Robert H. Abzug and Stephen E. Maizlish (Lexington: University Press of Kentucky, 1986), 53–64; and William Freehling, *The Road to Disunion* (New York: Oxford University Press, 1990). James Rawley, *Race and Politics* (Philadelphia: Lippincott, 1969), focuses on Kansas and the coming of the Civil War. In *Slavery and the American West,* Morrison argues that Republicans saw the Kansas conflict as a metaphor for an extension of the conflict between free and slave societies. Gabor S. Boritt, ed., *Why the Civil War Came* (New York: Oxford University Press, 1996), in an essay entitled "Abra-

ham Lincoln and the Question of Indentured Responsibility" (95–134), presses the point that the argument over slavery in the Kansas Territory, where slavery did not exist, in practice was a subterfuge for arguing over slavery where it did exist—in the South.

2. New York *Herald,* Dec. 21, 1857.

3. Morrison stresses this point in *Slavery and the American West.* Before this, and in other areas acquiring territorial status, settlers would move on to land that was not yet surveyed and had no form of government or laws. To protect their land claims and try to avoid violence, they would establish extralegal organizations such as claim clubs. Paul W. Gates, *Forty Million Acres* (Ithaca: Cornell University Press, 1954).

4. Memphis *Appeal,* Dec. 16, 1857.

5. Memphis *Appeal,* Dec. 21, 1857.

6. Memphis *Appeal,* Jan. 1, 1858.

7. Cincinnati *Enquirer,* Dec. 27, 1857.

8. Washington *Evening Star,* Jan. 4, 1958.

9. New York *Herald,* Dec. 23, 1857.

10. New York *Herald,* Dec. 26, 1857.

11. St. Louis *Missouri Democrat,* Dec. 25, 1857.

12. Philadelphia *Press,* Dec. 15, 1857.

13. Philadelphia *Press,* Dec. 16, 1857, emphasis in the original.

14. Philadelphia *Press,* Feb. 18, 1858.

15. Indianapolis *Journal,* Dec. 22, 24, 1857.

16. Indianapolis *Journal,* Dec. 28, 1857.

17. Chicago *Tribune,* Dec. 19, 1857.

18. New York *Tribune,* Dec. 21, 1857.

Chapter 5: John Brown's Raid

1. John Brown was controversial, both in his own time and as an historical figure. Among the most useful accounts of his life are James M. Malin, *John Brown and the Legend of Fifty-six* (Philadelphia: American Philosophical Society, 1942), in which Malin notes that Brown, at least in Kansas, played only a minor role. Malin also insists that the New York *Tribune,* which had sent a correspondent to Kansas, was guilty of sensationalism and falsification of the news. In *Bleeding Kansas* (New York: Oxford University Press, 1954), Alice Nichols ascribes a somewhat greater role in Kansas to Brown and observes that he was one of a very few abolitionists in that territory. Stephen B. Oates's *To Purge This Land with Blood: A Biography of John Brown* (New York: Harper and Row, 1970) stresses Brown's puritanism and his troubled business and personal life. Oates offers no definitive evidence regarding a Harpers Ferry conspiracy. In *His Soul Goes Marching On: Responses to John Brown and the Harpers Ferry Raid,* ed. Paul Finkelman (Charlottesville: University of Virginia Press, 1995), Finkelman argues in the Introduction (3) that northerners saw Brown variously as an antislavery saint, a brave but foolish extremist, or a lunatic. In that same volume Paul Knupfer ("A Crisis of Conservatism: Northern Unionists and the Harper's Ferry Raid") notes, "All sides in the discussion, regardless of party affiliation assumed a direct link between violent speech and violent behavior and worked with the same definition of fanaticism; attachment to one idea or principle at the expense of a realistic, reasoned understanding of the plurality of ends in public life" (141).

2. Oates, *To Purge This Land with Blood,* provides the best narration of what happened.

3. Washington *Evening Star,* Oct. 18, 1859.

4. Memphis *Appeal,* Oct. 21, 1859.

5. Memphis *Appeal,* Oct. 25, 1859.

6. New Orleans *Crescent,* Oct. 22, 1859.

7. New Orleans *Crescent,* Nov. 1, 1859.

8. Nashville *Whig,* Oct. 25, 1859.

9. Ibid.

10. Raleigh *Register,* Dec. 3, 1859.

11. Richmond *Enquirer,* Oct. 25, 1859, emphasis added.

12. New York *Herald,* Oct. 19, 1859.

13. New York *Herald,* Oct. 21, 1859.

14. Philadelphia *Press,* Oct. 19, 1859, emphasis in the original.

15. Philadelphia *Press,* Oct. 27, 1859.

16. Philadelphia *Press,* Nov. 7, 1859.

17. Cincinnati *Enquirer,* Oct. 18, 1859.

18. Cincinnati *Enquirer,* Oct. 22, 1859.

19. Albany *Evening Journal,* Oct. 20, 1859.

20. Ibid.

21. New York *Tribune,* Nov. 24, 1859.

22. New York *Tribune,* Nov. 29, 1859.

23. Harrisburg *Telegraph,* Dec. 21, 1859.

24. Chicago *Tribune,* Oct. 21, 1859.

25. Indianapolis *Journal,* Oct. 24, 1859.

26. Milwaukee *Daily Free Democrat,* Oct. 25, 1859.

27. Milwaukee *Daily Free Democrat,* Nov. 3, 1859.

Chapter 6: Lincoln's Election

1. James L. Huston, "Property Rights in Slavery and the Coming of Civil War," *Journal of Southern History* 65 (May 1999): 249–86, argues that southern fear of the loss of slave property, valued in the billions of dollars, was the key to understanding why southerners acted as they did. Huston dismisses the argument offered here and elsewhere that republican principles were important. Our research in newspapers, although revealing great interest and concern about that "property," does not convince us that it was the key issue. To the extent that it did matter, it was in the context of defense of republican principles in general. Defense of the Republic may now seem irrational, but that should not lead us to dismiss the issue.

2. Washington *National Intelligencer,* Nov. 8, 1860.

3. Washington *National Intelligencer,* Nov. 14, 1860.

4. Washington *National Intelligencer,* Mar. 7, 1861.

5. Abraham Lincoln, "Speech at the First Lincoln-Douglas Debate" (Ottawa, Ill., Aug. 21, 1858), quoted in Abraham Lincoln, *The Essential Abraham Lincoln,* ed. John Gabriel Hunt (New York: Gramercy Books, 1996), 129.

6. Robert Johannsen, *Stephen A. Douglas* (New York: Oxford University Press, 1973).

7. *Memphis Appeal,* Oct. 26, 1860.

8. New Orleans *Bee,* Oct. 23, 1860. This newspaper published both English and French editions.

9. New Orleans *Bee,* Nov. 8, 1860.

10. New Orleans *Bee,* Dec. 21, 1860.

11. New Orleans *Bee,* Feb. 27, 28, 1861.

12. Nashville *Whig,* Oct. 25, 1859.

13. Richmond *Enquirer,* Nov. 8, 1860, quoted in *Southern Editorials on Secession; Washington to Coolidge: A Documentary Record of Editorial Leadership and Criticism, 1785–1927,* ed. Dwight Lowell Dumond (New York, Century, 1931), 1:223.

14. Augusta *Daily Constitutionalist,* Nov. 16, 1860, quoted in *Southern Editorials on Secession,* ed. Dumond, 1:242.

15. Richmond *Enquirer,* Nov. 25, 1860.

16. Gallatin *Examiner,* Dec. 1, 1860, quoted in *Southern Editorials on Secession,* ed. Dumond, 1:286.

17. Charleston *Courier,* Nov. 1, 1860, quoted in Allan Nevins, *American Press Opinion* (Port Washington: D.C. Heath, 1969), 1:245–46. Stories of abolitionists burning towns circulated across Texas in 1860, although no evidence suggests that they were true.

18. Charleston *Courier,* Nov. 1, 1860, quoted in Nevins, *American Press Opinion,* 246.

19. Charleston *Courier,* Nov. 8, 1860.

20. New York *Herald,* Nov. 14, 1860.

21. New York *Herald,* Mar. 1, 1861.

22. Cincinnati *Enquirer,* Nov. 2, 1860.

23. Cincinnati *Enquirer,* Nov. 14, 1860.

24. Philadelphia *Press,* Oct. 26, 1860.

25. Ibid.

26. Philadelphia *Press,* Nov. 12, 1860.

27. Philadelphia *Press,* Dec. 30, 1860.

28. New York *Tribune,* Nov. 4, 1860.

29. New York *Tribune,* Nov. 6, 1860.

30. Indianapolis *Journal,* Nov. 10, 1860.

31. St. Louis *Missouri Democrat,* Nov. 1, 1860.

32. New York *Tribune,* Nov. 26, 1860.

33. New York *Tribune,* Jan. 10, 1861.

Chapter 7: Firing on Fort Sumter

1. The story of the events that led to the firing on Fort Sumter, including the dissension within Lincoln's government, is told best by Richard W. Current, *Lincoln and the First Shot* (Philadelphia: J. B. Lippincott, 1963). Current places some of the blame for critical confusion on William Seward and maintains that the confusion might have caused Jefferson Davis's miscalculation about the northern response to Confederate demands that all federal soldiers leave the South. Seward spread rumors that Lincoln, despite what he said in his inaugural speech, would abandon the forts and not force collection of fees in southern ports. Current also asserts that the Confederates believed that northern Democrats, if the federal government attacked the South, would then join with the South. In effect, any war would be between the parties and not the sections.

Lincoln wanted peace, but for one united country. Davis wanted peace for two separate countries. In *Days of Defiance,* Klein covers much the same ground as does Current. Klein's account makes even more clear the lack of a carefully reasoned strategy on either side and the role of the press in dramatizing the conflict as it unfolded.

2. Providence *Daily Post* quoted in Perkins, *Northern Editorials on Secession,* 2:443.

3. New York *Herald* quoted in Perkins, *Northern Editorials on Secession,* 2:455.

4. Hartford *Daily Times* quoted in Perkins, *Northern Editorials on Secession,* 2:377.

5. New York *Tribune,* Apr. 15, 1861.

6. New York *Tribune,* Apr. 17, 18, 22, 1861.

7. New York *Herald,* Apr. 8, 1861.

8. New York *Herald* quoted in Nevins, *American Press Opinion,* 252–53.

9. Cincinnati *Enquirer,* Apr. 18, 1861.

10. New Orleans *Bee,* Apr. 5, 1861.

11. Savannah *Morning News,* Apr. 15, 1861.

12. St. Louis *Missouri Republican,* Apr. 19, 1861, quoted in *Southern Editorials on Secession,* ed. Dumond, 1:500.

13. Washington *National Intelligencer,* Apr. 13, 1861.

14. Boston *Herald,* Apr. 15, 1861, quoted in Perkins, *Northern Editorials on Secession,* 2:729.

15. Boston *Post* quoted in Perkins, *Northern Editorials on Secession,* 2:740.

16. Detroit *Free Press,* Apr. 29, 1861, quoted in Perkins, *Northern Editorials on Secession,* 2:753.

17. New York *Journal of Commerce,* May 6, 1861, quoted in Perkins, *Northern Editorials on Secession,* 2:759–60.

18. Ibid.

19. Columbus *Daily Capitol City Fact* quoted in Perkins, *Northern Editorials on Secession,* 2:837.

20. Springfield *Republican* quoted in Perkins, *Northern Editorials on Secession,* 2:1064–65.

21. Providence *Daily Journal,* Apr. 26, 1861, quoted in Perkins, *Northern Editorials on Secession,* 2:1067.

22. Boston *Transcript,* May 10, 1861, quoted in Perkins, *Northern Editorials on Secession,* 2:1082; Albany *Evening Journal,* June 1, 1861, quoted in Perkins, *Northern Editorials on Secession,* 2:1089–90.

23. Louisville *Daily Courier,* Apr. 18, 1861, quoted in *Southern Editorials on Secession,* ed. Dumond, 1:494.

24. St. Louis *Missouri Republican,* Apr. 19, 1861.

25. Raleigh *Standard,* Apr. 20, 1861, quoted in *Southern Editorials on Secession,* ed. Dumond, 1:505.

26. Nashville *Daily Patriot,* Apr. 24, 1861, quoted in *Southern Editorials on Secession,* ed. Dumond, 1:509.

27. Nashville *Republican Banner,* May 9, 1861.

Conclusion

1. Benedict O'G. Anderson, *Imagined Communities: Reflections on the Origin and Spread of Nationalism* (New York: Verso Press, 1991).

2. Thomas Gustafson, *Representative Words: Politics, Literature, and the American Lan-*

guage, 1776–1865 (New York: Cambridge University Press, 1992), makes a convincing case for the power of words in shaping the American republic and describes well the ways "people [were] playing language games, stealing symbols. . . , working the loom of language to reweave the fabric of imperatives" (13). Gustafson also offers explanation of how, in the post-Revolutionary era, men such as James Madison and James Fenimore Cooper "worried that the greatest danger to the republic is the ease with which false representation can masquerade as true representation" (22). Gustafson contends that by the 1850s a sense of conformity concerning the use of key words in the American community broke down and thus threatened moral and political stability. He also notes, "Just like a politician, words are motivated by interests; they respond to constituencies of power, they cannot be trusted to speak the same thing to different audiences" (317). Certainly, the words that appeared in newspapers from 1856 to 1861 did not speak the same thing to all audiences.

3. Walter Lippmann, *Public Opinion* (New York: Harcourt Brace, 1922).

4. Michael Ignatieff, *The Warrior's Honor: Ethnic War and the Modern Conscience* (New York: Metropolitan Books, 1997), 27.

INDEX

Abbott and Winans (news-gathering service), 18
abolition/abolitionists: American Colonization Society, 2–3; Beecher family, 44; efforts to end cause, 3; as fanatics, 33, 51, 58, 94; John Brown as free-soiler, 71–73; movement and newspapers, *see* abolitionist press; northern press descriptions, 38, 40; southern press descriptions, 47–48, 58, 75–76; Sumner antislavery speeches, 34–36
abolitionist press: *Liberator,* 3, 25; violence against, 3, 22–23, 24–27
Adams, John Quincy, 23
American Colonization Society, 2–3
American Telegraph Company, 17
Anti-Masonic Party, 51
Appeal (Memphis, Tenn.): on Douglas candidacy, 91; on *Dred Scott* decision, 57; on Fort Sumter attack, 107; on impending Civil War, 107; on John Brown's raid, 75–76; on Lecompton Constitution, 63–64; on Lincoln candidacy, 91
Associated Press (AP): and *Dred Scott* case, 50; impact of, 17–18; ownership of, 17

Baldasty, Gerald, 10
Bee (New Orleans, La.): on Fort Sumter attack, 108, 114; on impending Civil War, 107–8; on Lincoln candidacy, 91–92; on Lincoln presidency, 92; on North-South differences, 32; on secession, 92
Beecher, Henry Ward, 44
Bell, John: presidential candidacy (1860) of, 77, 88, 91
Bennett, James Gordon: on Brooks-Sumner incident, 45; on *Dred Scott* decision, 55–56; on Fort Sumter attack, 106–7; growth of *Herald* (New York), 10–11, 12, 15–16, 20, 23, 31;

on John Brown's raid, 78; on Lecompton Constitution, 64–65; on Lincoln candidacy/presidency, 95–96; on slavery issue, 45
Birney, James G., 25
Black Republicans: "bleeding Kansas" and, 49, 61; and Lecompton Constitution, 64, 78; Lincoln as, 87–88, 90–91, 93, 98; southern press on, 80; use of term, 57
Booth, Sherman: on *Dred Scott* case, 54–55; on John Brown's raid, 83–84
Bowles, Samuel, 10–11, 29
Breckinridge, John C., 86, 111, 112
Brooks, Preston: caning of Sumner, 35; as fire-eater, 37, 44. *See also* Brooks-Sumner incident
Brooks-Sumner incident, 4, 34–48; content of Sumner speech, 35–36; Democratic press on, 37, 44–48; northern press on, 39–41, 42–45; as North-South symbol, 37; Republican press on, 37–38, 39–40, 43–44, 48; southern press on, 41–42, 45–48; Whig press on, 48
Brown, John. *See* John Brown's raid
Buchanan, James: and Lecompton Constitution, 61–63, 65, 68, 79
Burlingame, Anson, 41
Burns, Anthony, 73
Butler, Andrew, 36
bylines: development of, 11

capitalization: and growth of press, 10, 20
Chase, Salmon, 79
civil libel, 24
Civil War, outbreak of. *See* Fort Sumter attack
Clay, Cassius Marcellus, 27
Clay, Henry, 76
Commercial Bulletin (St. Louis, Mo.), 26
competition: and growth of press, 11, 17–18,

LORMAN A. RATNER is professor of history emeritus, University of Tennessee, and adjunct professor of history at the University of Illinois at Urbana-Champaign. Among his books relating to the subject of this volume are *Powderkeg: Northern Opposition to the Antislavery Movement, 1831–1840* and *James Kirke Paulding: The Last Republican.*

DWIGHT L. TEETER JR. is professor of journalism at the University of Tennessee. He is coauthor, with Jean Folkerts, of *Voices of a Nation: A History of the Mass Media in the United States* and, with Bill Loving, *Law of Mass Communications: Freedom and Control of Print and Broadcast Media.*

Selling Free Enterprise: The Business Assault on Labor and Liberalism, 1945–60   *Elizabeth A. Fones-Wolf*

Last Rights: Revisiting *Four Theories of the Press*   *Edited by John C. Nerone*

"We Called Each Other Comrade": Charles H. Kerr & Company, Radical Publishers   *Allen Ruff*

WCFL, Chicago's Voice of Labor, 1926–78   *Nathan Godfried*

Taking the Risk Out of Democracy: Corporate Propaganda versus Freedom and Liberty   *Alex Carey; edited by Andrew Lohrey*

Media, Market, and Democracy in China: Between the Party Line and the Bottom Line   *Yuezhi Zhao*

Print Culture in a Diverse America   *Edited by James P. Danky and Wayne A. Wiegand*

The Newspaper Indian: Native American Identity in the Press, 1820–90   *John M. Coward*

E. W. Scripps and the Business of Newspapers   *Gerald J. Baldasty*

Picturing the Past: Media, History, and Photography   *Edited by Bonnie Brennen and Hanno Hardt*

Rich Media, Poor Democracy: Communication Politics in Dubious Times   *Robert W. McChesney*

Silencing the Opposition: Antinuclear Movements and the Media in the Cold War   *Andrew Rojecki*

Citizen Critics: Literary Public Spheres   *Rosa A. Eberly*

Communities of Journalism: A History of American Newspapers and Their Readers   *David Paul Nord*

From Yahweh to Yahoo!: The Religious Roots of the Secular Press   *Doug Underwood*

The Struggle for Control of Global Communication: The Formative Century   *Jill Hills*

Fanatics and Fire-eaters: Newspapers and the Coming of the Civil War   *Lorman A. Ratner and Dwight L. Teeter Jr.*

The University of Illinois Press
is a founding member of the
Association of American University Presses.

Composed in 9/13 ITC Stone Serif
with ITC Stone Sans display
by Celia Shapland
for the University of Illinois Press
Designed by Paula Newcomb
Manufactured by Thomson-Shore, Inc.

University of Illinois Press
1325 South Oak Street
Champaign, IL 61820-6903
www.press.uillinois.edu